E P I P H A N Y

**INTERPRETING
THE LESSONS OF
THE CHURCH YEAR**

DAVID M. RHOADS

**PROCLAMATION 5
SERIES B**

FORTRESS PRESS   MINNEAPOLIS

PROCLAMATION 5
Interpreting the Lessons of the Church Year
Series B, Epiphany

The author wishes to express his gratitude to Sandy Roberts and Steve Samuelson for reading the manuscript and for giving valuable suggestions to help make this material more readable and more useful for sermon preparation.

Cover design: Spangler Design Team

Library of Congress Cataloging-in-Publication Data
(Revised for Ser. B, v. 1-4)

Proclamation 5.

   Contents: ser. A. [2] Epiphany / Pheme Perkins —
[etc.] — ser. B. [1] Advent/Christmas / William H.
Willimon — [2] Epiphany / David Rhoads — [3] Lent /
Thomas Hoyt, Jr. — [4] Holy Week / Walter Wink.
   1. Bible—Homiletical use.   2. Bible—Liturgical
lessons, English.   I. Perkins, Pheme.
BS534.5.P765   1993   251   92-22973
ISBN 0-8006-4185-X (ser. B, Advent/Christmas)
ISBN 0-8006-4186-8 (ser. B, Epiphany)
ISBN 0-8006-4187-6 (ser. B, Lent)
ISBN 0-8006-4188-4 (ser. B, Holy Week)

The paper used in this publication meets the minimum requirements of American National Standard for Information Sciences—Permanence of Paper for Printed Library Materials, ANSI Z329.48-1984.   ∞™

Manufactured in the U.S.A.   AF 1-4186

97   96   95   94   93   1   2   3   4   5   6   7   8   9   10

CONTENTS

The Epiphany of Our Lord

Lutheran	Roman Catholic	Episcopal	Common Lectionary
Isa. 60:1-6	Isa. 60:1-6	Isa. 60:1-6, 9	Isa. 60:1-6
Eph. 3:2-12	Eph. 3:2-3a, 5-6	Eph. 3:1-12	Eph. 3:1-12
Matt. 2:1-12	Matt. 2:1-12	Matt. 2:1-12	Matt. 2:1-12

FIRST LESSON: ISAIAH 60:1-9

This poetic vision in Third Isaiah echoes Second Isaiah. At the time of the exile, Second Isaiah announced the Lord's promise to restore Israelites to the land. Now they have returned to the land, but the glorious visions of Second Isaiah have not come to pass. The land is devastated, the walls of Jerusalem are not rebuilt, the temple is in ruins, and the people are disillusioned. Seeking to deliver the people from despair, Isaiah here recalls Israelites to a life of righteousness in order that they might fulfill their vocation in God's plan for all humanity.

The vision is this: Yahweh will shine upon them like the breaking of dawn. In turn, their reflection of God's glory will be so luminous that the nations in darkness will be drawn to their light. The nations will flock to Israel, like one moving from darkness toward dawn. The merchants of the earth will bring sacrifices for worship. They will bring the wealth of the nations on long caravans of camels, tribute that will restore the city walls and rebuild the temple. They will submit freely to the light of justice that Israel provides for the nations. Then Israel will live in peace. There will no longer be any external threat, because the possibility of war will have disappeared. There will no longer be any internal threat, because the nation will live in righteousness. Isaiah's vision empowered the people to live out their calling in righteousness and in the confidence that God had not abandoned them.

SECOND LESSON: EPHESIANS 3:1-12

The mystery that the author of Ephesians is talking about is this: God is forming Jews and Gentiles into one new humanity. Under the old order a dividing wall existed. To become part of God's people, it was necessary to come before God as a Jew—to become circumcised and to follow the law. But all along God had a plan, which is now revealed in Jesus. In the new order, Jews and Gentiles alike come before God based on faith in

4

Jesus. Being Jewish is not an advantage, and being Gentile is not a disadvantage. Gentiles are equal partners, coheirs of all God's promises to Israel. Gone is the basis on which Jews remained isolated and Gentiles were excluded. All grounds for hostility, boasting, and alienation have been removed, for God is creating one new humanity to encompass all groups previously divided.

According to this passage, God's goal in history is to unify all humanity. The death and resurrection of Jesus are the key events in human history, for they have enabled this unification of humanity. By justifying all freely, God has placed all humans on the same sure footing before God. The cross thus removed any basis for the dominance of one group over another— Jews and Greeks, slave and free, male and female. The cross removed all cultural barriers while at the same time preserving all cultures. The announcement of this reconciliation is not an abstract idea but a powerful word that transforms relationships between people of different cultures, nations, and languages. God wills to bring all people to this unifying experience (knowledge) of salvation.

The mystery is more than a plan or an insight. It is a force in history— the Creator bringing the created order to consummation by grace. In a sense the mystery is Jesus—the announcement of his redemption, the power of his resurrection—a force powerful enough to transform humanity. The "wisdom" of the mystery is that God is bringing about the plan not by coercion but by the persuasion of grace. God has made peace by removing all barriers to reconcilation with God and among humans.

The mystery is concrete—manifest in the personal, historical, cultural, and social realities of the world. In the church God has displayed this new humanity by incorporating all peoples, cultures, languages, and nations. This mystery is so wondrous that Paul's life has become a doxology. The author presents Paul as one who gladly endures suffering for the enactment of this mystery, because such a reality is worth living and dying for.

GOSPEL: MATTHEW 2:1-12

The various nativity stories in Matthew show that the birth of Jesus inaugurates a new age in history. Matthew's birth stories are about the "genesis" of Jesus Christ (1:1). As the Spirit hovered at creation, the Spirit now overshadows Mary, enabling her to conceive. Jesus' birth begins a new epoch in a series of epochs of fourteen generations each. Each episode in the birth stories brings a scriptural promise to fulfillment. Some episodes replicate events in Israel's history—a sojourn in Egypt, dreams from God, the killing of children. The guiding star signals the epiphany of Jesus, who heralds a new era.

5

The setting encompasses the larger world of the East from which the Gentile wise men have traveled. The immediate setting is Israel, an agricultural society with two classes—a small ruling elite of landowners and an overwhelming majority of peasants. The star, bringing heavenly guidance, comes to rest over not the powerful rulers in Jerusalem but over the rural village of Nazareth.

Herod ruled the Jewish kingdom on behalf of the Romans. He exacted high taxes and hard labor from the people in order to erect Roman buildings and cities in Israel. In a demented state at the end of his life, Herod put to death members of his family out of fear that they were plotting against him. No other historical documentation exists to verify that Herod killed the children of Bethlehem. Matthew's depiction of him, however, is obviously not out of character.

The episode depicts Herod living out the fears of the old age. Herod is troubled because a king from the people poses a threat. He lies to the wise men about wanting to worship Jesus. He is angry when the wise men do not fall for his ploy, and he gives orders to kill the infants of Bethlehem. He wields the power of death to preserve his rule and passes on the tactics of domination to his sons. Herod foreshadows the whole line of Jewish leaders in the Gospel, who also use weapons of power against Jesus.

Under King Herod there arose King Jesus. Jesus is at the center of this story even though he is offstage most of the time. His appearance attracts an international audience and threatens the king whose rule is based on fear and domination. God's choice for king is born in the village of Bethlehem. He is called Immanuel, meaning "God with us." He is called Jesus, because "he saves" his people from their sins. As ruler, he will "shepherd" his people Israel.

Other figures in the birth narratives also display the traits of those who belong to the new age. The righteous Joseph intends to divorce his betrothed quietly out of concern for her, rather than to exercise his right to exact a severe punishment for her apparent offense. The wise men sincerely want to give homage to the new king. They follow wherever the star of God leads, experience great joy when they find the infant, and present gifts. They trust even Herod, but they are warned in a dream not to return to him. The wise men foreshadow those who respond favorably to Jesus throughout Matthew's Gospel, and they anticipate the mission to the nations (28:16-20).

Two cautions. First, the Gospels have a tendency to stereotype the followers of Jesus as being all good and the Jewish leaders as being all evil. The character types in Matthew are meant to lead us to deal with the good and evil character traits in ourselves and do not accurately depict Jewish leaders, as we see when we read about them in other sources. We must, therefore, be careful not to use this or any Gospel in the service of anti-Semitism by perpetuating stereotypes offered in the story. Second, we need to counter the patriarchal orientation of these ancient texts. Matthew's narrative is clearly centered around male roles. Women are subordinate and peripheral. Nevertheless, the women—Mary and others referred to in the genealogy—represent the common folk from whom Jesus comes.

HOMILETICAL REFLECTIONS

Epiphanies are manifestations of God in the world, the reality of God in human events. The concept of epiphany has many symbols—light that attracts, a mystery that has allure, a vision that transforms. Although it is possible to make abstractions about epiphanies, they are quite concrete— the presence of justice, the movement of a star, the birth of an infant, the reconciliation of enemies, the writing of a Gospel, the penning of a letter, and a vision of new life. All of these witness to the central epiphany that the Feast of Epiphany celebrates, the manifestation of God in Jesus Christ.

Epiphanies harbinger the new: a new Israel, a new age, a secret newly revealed, a new Messiah. That was two thousand years ago. Yet when the stories are told again and the power of God is unleashed anew, the transformations and reconciliations are like chain reactions from the release of atomic energy. The experience is new and fresh, as though God were doing it for the first time.

The epiphanies of the Bible can help us recognize epiphanies in the present. In order to recognize true epiphanies, we can beware not to equate epiphanies with human successes—possessions we accumulate, achievements that bring us notoriety and admiration, victory over another. Rather, biblical epiphanies usually emerge from deprivation and places of marginalization—an impoverished nation recently conquered, a peasant from Galilee, the loss of children, a Jew who used to persecute Christians, the crumbling of dreams. At the absolute center of our faith is a crucified man who redeems the world. Such manifestations of God undercut worldly achievement and prevent us from mistaking God's actions for human glories. They also lead us to see everything differently.

The experience of an epiphany is by nature transforming. There are no disinterested observers, because it is precisely those who have eyes to see (or who are given eyes to see) who experience them. Thus epiphanies elicit responses, a new purpose in life: a prophetic vision unleashes the impulse to justice; the enactment of true justice inspires allegiance; a star leads sages on a pilgrimage; the death of Jesus impels Paul to embark on a worldwide mission of reconciliation. The biblical stories themselves have taken countless generations in their grasp. Epiphanies are therefore transforming events. The season of Epiphany allows us to see and be changed.

Epiphanies lead us to look beyond narrow loyalties to a worldwide vision: Israel will be a light to the nations; sages come from the East; Paul proclaims an end to hostility between Jew and Gentile. Epiphanies enable us to transcend our narrow vision and embrace God's point of view. God cares about the whole world and offers a vision of world salvation. Socrates said he was a citizen not of Athens or of Greece but of the world. In response to the breakup of Czechoslovakia into two separate states, President Václav Havel said, "The fact in itself that two states should emerge out of one is not a tragedy. . . . I do not place the highest value on the state, but on humanity."

Similarly followers of Jesus have a sense of purpose that goes beyond the narrow allegiance to the family, the place of work, the corporation, the nation, an economic system. The epiphanies of the Christian life impel us to a larger allegiance to the kingdom of God. That allegiance frees us to be humane in all we do. We carry out our tasks at home or in business with a larger vision. Common sense may tell us simply to look out for ourselves and our own, but God has a larger purpose in mind. We are called to be part of that.

The manifestations of God in the world address the worst human hostilities. We may ask what will break the irreconcilable enmity in Northern Ireland, the hostility between the Serbs and the Croats, the Israelis and the Palestinians, the blacks and whites in South Africa, and on and on. We live in an age when ethnic, racial, and national groups are taking new pride in their identities and are fiercely recovering and defending them. This situation shows great promise for the preservation of cultural diversity, but it also holds many dangers.

The ancient writers were no strangers to bitter human conflicts. Isaiah's vision comes to people recovering from a devastating conquest of the whole nation and the terrifying experience of exile. Jesus is born in the kingdom of a man who slaughters infants. Paul stands against the oppressive systems of the ancient world—male over female, Greek over Jew, free over slave. The early church was convinced that the power of God manifest in the life, death, and resurrection of Jesus was an unsurpassed force in the world, powerful enough to heal the pain of hatred and to mold communities of love. Paul's own epiphany transformed one who killed Christians into one ready to die for the Lord. The story of the Jewish Messiah who absorbed hostility and did not return it even in death crumbled the dividing wall of hostility.

The texts articulate the kind of leadership we need for an age that will engender peace. Observe the contrast in the Gospel lesson. Herod dominates and Jesus shepherds. Herod excludes and Jesus includes. Herod lords over and Jesus empowers. The Roman Catholic Church in Brazil, in seeking to make the church (and the society) more democratic, goes beyond a definition of democracy as a system that ensures certain equal rights for everyone. "In a democracy," a Bible study leader declared, "the community is organized actively to involve everyone in meaningful expressions of ministry, especially the marginalized." Here is an adequate description of the kingdom of God. Here is an adequate understanding of the role of the leader as one who bears God's concern for inclusion and reconciliation.

The Baptism of Our Lord
First Sunday after the Epiphany

Lutheran	Roman Catholic	Episcopal	Common Lectionary
Isa. 42:1-7	Isa. 42:1-4, 6-7	Isa. 42:1-9	Gen. 1:1-5
Acts 10:34-38	Acts 10:34-38	Acts 10:34-38	Acts 19:1-7
Mark 1:4-11	Mark 1:7-11	Mark 1:7-11	Mark 1:4-11

FIRST LESSON: ISAIAH 42:1-7

This is the first of four Servant Songs of Second Isaiah. The Israelites are in captivity in Babylon. They have experienced great humiliation, and in exile they no longer hold to the covenant relationship with God. Yet even if they no longer uphold God, God nevertheless upholds them. God has not forgotten them. God is still loyal to them. God still delights in them as the chosen people.

Despite its humiliating captivity, Israel is called by the God of heaven and earth to a historic task as agent for the restoration of the world. Israel is still to be the servant of God, obedient to God's commands, executive agent of God's power, and anointed with the Spirit to carry out the task. The people of Israel in "servitude" in Babylon are called to be "servants" of the nations, to show God's justice before all the nations.

Israel will not gain prominence in a new world order by violent domination, by crushing people. Israel will not harm the least of any society, will not break a bruised reed or quench a dimly burning wick, will not make loud proclamations in the streets. Rather, by persistent acts of justice, Israel will gain a reputation for justice to the farthest coastlands. Israel will set right the relations with God and among nations. In the end Israel will come to be served by the nations, because all nations will honor Israel for establishing justice on the earth.

In God's ongoing creative activity, Israel itself will be God's covenant with the nations. Israel will also be light to the nations, to bring those who are without sight, those in darkness and captivity, into the light of God's justice. Israel itself is in blindness and captivity to a foreign nation, and yet God calls Israel to be the means of sight and release for the nations. Wonders never cease. In the midst of captivity and futility, God calls the nation to a vital vocation.

10

SECOND LESSON: ACTS 10:34-38

This text is a sermon within a story of baptism. To understand the text, we need to understand the context. Acts 10 is the amazing story of the conversion of the first Gentile. The Holy Spirit orchestrates the whole event. First, Peter has a vision showing all things to be "clean." Then Cornelius, a Roman centurion, has a vision leading him to summon Peter. After a lengthy journey, Peter enters this "unclean" house of a Gentile. Each explains how he had come to this meeting, and then Peter preaches. His brief sermon is typical of the earlier sermons in Acts: proclamation, scriptural proof, and a call to repentance. It also contains the statement, only now fully dawning on Peter, that God is no respecter of persons.

The sermon opens and closes with the key point that God is not partial, does not discriminate. The earliest Christians assumed that to become a follower of Jesus one became a Jew. Gentiles had always been purified and circumcised in order to be acceptable as God's people. Would the requirement not be the same for Gentiles to become followers of Jesus? Would they not become Jews who followed Jesus? But now God has declared to Peter that all things are clean, that God will accept from all nations those who fear God (show honor and awe toward God) and do what is right (repent and live for righteousness). The entire Jewish legal basis that defined membership in God's elect shifted from under these early Christians. God is not partial to Israel but accepts all. People need only repent, and they will be forgiven.

The sermon reveals the shift to a universal salvation. Jesus was the Christ of the Jews, but in his resurrection he has become Lord of all nations. Although he was executed in Judea, he was raised to be judge of all, living and dead. Although only a few Jews witnessed his ministry and resurrection, Jesus commissioned them to proclaim that all who believe in Jesus will receive forgiveness of sins. The message Jesus Christ brought to Israel was a message of peace (with people inside and outside the nation). After John's baptism, Jesus was anointed with the Holy Spirit and power, and he went about doing good and healing all oppressed by the devil. This Holy Spirit was available to Israel through Jesus and is now available to all nations through the apostles.

While Peter is still speaking, the Holy Spirit comes upon Cornelius and his family, and they begin to speak in tongues and to praise God (10:44-48). The circumcised believers are amazed that the Spirit has come to people who are not circumcised, and they proceed to baptize them with water. This is the Pentecost for Gentiles—the Spirit made available not only to Jews from every nation but now also to Gentiles from every nation. In Peter's sermon, God is the major actor. It is God who does not discriminate, preaches peace through Jesus, anoints Jesus with the Spirit and power, raises him from the dead, chooses the Twelve as witnesses, ordains Jesus as judge, and forgives sins in Jesus' name. Also, in Luke's depiction, Jesus' baptism was the formative event in his ministry. Jesus was anointed with the Holy Spirit and power to preach peace, to go about doing good, and to heal all oppressed by the devil. The whole point of the sermon is that, as a result of Jesus' life, death, and resurrection, Gentiles such as Cornelius can now receive the Holy Spirit and power. He too can preach peace, go about doing good, and heal all oppressed by the devil— just as Jesus and Peter had done.

GOSPEL: MARK 1:4-11

Here is Mark's account of Jesus' baptism. Notice how Mark's entire introduction (1:1-12) portrays the Gospel as God's story (as with the story of Cornelius). God is establishing rulership over the world. God gives the prophecy to Isaiah, sends John, forgives sins, opens the heavens, anoints Jesus with the Spirit, declares him to be the Son, and impels him into the wilderness. In turn, Jesus announces the good news about God: "The time has been fulfilled. The rule of God has arrived. Repent and trust the good news."

God chooses an unknown person from a small village (Nazareth) in a marginal region (Galilee). Jesus has no pedigree. He is not from the capital city and not a part of the ruling elite. Mark contains no birth narratives, and Jesus is not the Son of David. He is a peasant carpenter (6:1-6). God works on the margins to bring new life to the center. When Jesus comes up from the water, he has a private epiphany; he sees the heavens opened and the Spirit coming upon him. The Spirit empowers him to carry out his task as Messiah. Thus God grants authority apart from the official authorities.

The voice from heaven declares, "You are my only son; I delighted in choosing you." This quotation is from two scriptural texts. The first part is from an enthronement Psalm (2:7), implicitly declaring Jesus to be the designated Messiah king ("my only son"). The second part is from a suffering servant passage (Isa. 42:1), indicating the kind of Messiah Jesus is to be. Jesus is given only this orientation for the "way of God" he is to follow. Beyond that he finds his way in response to the Spirit as he confronts problems and probes the extent of his authority.

The baptism is the origin of Jesus' identity and therefore of his independence. He will not follow the values of the culture: saving himself, seeking greatness, wanting power, lording over people, acting out of fear, being destructive. He will resist these because his purpose and authority come from God. He will follow the values of God: losing his life for others, relinquishing status, serving the people, acting out of faith, and bringing life. Jesus' life is rooted in the life of God. His identity comes from God and not from people.

Jesus' baptism is unique among baptisms. John baptized as a means to forgive sins. For Jesus, however, John's baptism anointed him to be the agent to usher in God's rule. Jesus in turn would baptize others in the Holy Spirit. Jesus' baptism was thus the formative event by which God inaugurated the divine rule.

HOMILETICAL REFLECTIONS

The baptisms in these texts demonstrate that epiphanies are "identifying moments" that reveal who God is and who we are.

1. Epiphanies reveal who God is, because epiphanies are God-centered. God initiates them. God reveals the divine nature in them. A key characteristic of God's identity in the epiphanies of these texts is that God does not discriminate. God transcends ethnic identity and social class. In Acts a Galilean fisherman preaches to a Roman centurion, who does not lose his ethnic identity in becoming a Christian. As such, there is no normative Christian culture. God does not obliterate who we are—Jew or Gentile, female or male, management or labor, Asian American or African American. Rather God baptizes all these dimensions and transforms them into a new community. Baptism itself is incorporation into a community that relishes diverse ethnic, racial, gender, cultural, and economic differences and at the same time celebrates unity in the foundational story of our faith and in the Spirit who empowers all.

These texts also display a God who works through the marginalized, a divine characteristic that readers from a dominant culture might miss: The insignificant nation of Israel is God's people, Peter is a Galilean peasant, the Messiah is a Jewish carpenter. In *A Black Theology of Liberation* (Maryknoll, N.Y.: Orbis, 1986), James Cone shows us the blackness of God as the one who identifies with the suffering and the oppressed. In *Galilean Journey: The Mexican American Promise* (Maryknoll, N.Y.: Orbis, 1990), Virgilio Elizondo shows a correlation between Hispanic Americans and Galilean Jews as groups that are marginalized and oppressed in similar ways. If God brought salvation into the world through Galilean peasants, God also works through the unique spirit and insights of Hispanic Christians to bring greater peace and justice. Unless we are open to God's central work on the margins, we may miss God's work completely. After all, we worship a God who saves the world through one who was rejected and executed by his society.

2. Epiphanies also give identity to those who have epiphanies. Israel's experiences of God in history kept redefining its identity in terms of God's

call to Israel, not its continued apostasy. In Mark the baptism gave identity to Jesus as God's Son. Jesus had a vision, received the Spirit, heard the voice of God, and was led to confront Satan. This epiphany shaped Jesus' self-understanding and ministry. Cornelius too saw visions, heard the gospel from Peter, and received the empowering Spirit. This event would henceforth define Cornelius's life.

Many people have epiphanies, moments when the curtain seems to be drawn back, and they experience God. People are often reluctant to share these moments. Some Christians are suspicious of religious experiences. We are right not to absolutize them, but such experiences surely can be vehicles of divine manifestation, a powerful means of grace. Such events give depth and purpose to people's lives. In God's encounter with us, we find ourselves, our identity. We can lift up such epiphanies and relate them to the fullness of God as it unfolds in the Jesus event—the epiphany that defines us all.

We can also relate these epiphanies to baptism. Many modern Christians were baptized as infants and have no recollection of this foundational event. Through services of reaffirmation, we can remember when God claimed us as daughters and sons. We can pray for the continuing release in our lives of the Holy Spirit given at baptism. By recalling our baptism, we reinforce our identity as people of God, because baptism incorporates us into the company of the committed as a place of support for our identity in Christ.

We need the community of Christians in order to maintain our baptismal identity. We often seek our identity elsewhere, from a peer group or a skill or achievement or from a goal we hope to attain or a person we emulate. We allow the commercialism and the individualism of our age to define us. From movies, television, and sports, the superstars of the culture seek to provide our identity. We may place our identity in sexual appeal or youthfulness or health or financial security. Some of us have a negative self-identity, as a victim of abuse or as part of a group discriminated against by society or from the attitudes and expectations of others.

The gospel, by contrast, invites us to see our identity as made and redeemed by God. Here was a broken people in exile whom God called to be the means of salvation for the world. Here was a capable centurion with an important position whom God called to serve a power higher than the Roman Empire. Here was a carpenter from Galilee whom God anointed with power to redeem a world. God's claim on us is a powerful and secure basis for the autonomy of the self, for the self-esteem and inner motivation to be our own person for God. Nothing less will do. Neither our circumstances nor our achievements nor our ethnic group nor our family is ultimately the true source of our identity as human beings.

We speak of politicians who are not owned, not beholden to special interests or to self-interest. We speak of people who are their own persons, who have principles they will not compromise or commitments they will not break—regardless of the cost. Recall the strength of character of the Olympic runner in the film *Chariots of Fire*, who refused to race on the Sabbath despite the loss of a gold medal. Such self-possession is often rooted in the epiphanies wherein God has made a claim on us.

Such character strength is never rooted in self-righteousness or zealous triumphalism or fierce individualism. It is strength rooted in the security of God's love for us, strength that is beyond zealotry, strength that does not need to triumph, strength that brings no harm to the lowly of the earth, strength that will not break a bruised reed or crush a dimly burning wick. On the contrary, Christian self-possession is the self grasped by God, possessed by Jesus Christ—committed to living so that the bruised reed is strengthened and the dimly burning wick is fanned into brightness.

As such, the baptismal epiphanies of God authorize us for ministry. Jesus' baptism authorized him to exorcise demons, heal the sick, and pardon sins. Peter's baptism authorized him to proclaim. Recently a man entered a church in my town on a weekday seeking a priest to bless him. No pastor was present, but several women welcomed him and said, "In our church, everyone is a priest, and we will be glad to pray for your healing." And they did. In Brazil several uneducated laypeople expressed a reluctance to take part in worship leadership. "We are not priests," they protested. A bishop who was present replied, "But your baptism is your ordination into ministry. Don't let anyone or anything diminish the authority you received there." Baptism authorizes us for ministry in the church and for life in the world, authorizes us to serve, to foster justice and peace, to bring healing to a broken world.

Second Sunday after the Epiphany

Lutheran	Roman Catholic	Episcopal	Common Lectionary
1 Sam. 3:1-10	1 Sam. 3:3b-10, 19	1 Sam. 3:1-10	1 Sam. 3:1-10 (11-20)
1 Cor. 6:12-20	1 Cor. 6:13c-15a, 17-20	1 Cor. 6:11b-20	1 Cor. 6:12-20
John 1:43-51	John 1:35-42	John 1:43-51	John 1:35-42

FIRST LESSON: 1 SAMUEL 3:1-20

This story depicts a transition from the aged Eli to the young Samuel as spiritual leader of the people. Eli was a priest with a reputation for prophecy. Due to his age, Eli was no longer able to guard the sanctuary. That job was left to Samuel, a young trainee under Eli's tutelage. Samuel was neither the obvious nor the designated successor of Eli or of his household. The Lord appeared to a young trainee outside the established leadership. The story does not suggest that Samuel was dense or unable to discern the presence of the Lord. Rather visions were so rare that the event was unexpected.

Samuel was on watch toward morning. He was awake and heard someone address him. He kept thinking that the voice was Eli calling to him—ironic in light of the oracle to follow. On the third occasion, Eli, finally guessing the origin of the call, advised the boy to respond to the Lord. When Samuel did so, the Lord appeared to him and gave an oracle against the house of Eli for the blasphemy of Eli's sons. The doom on Eli's house was irrevocable; neither sacrifices nor offerings could avert it. Despite Samuel's reluctance, Eli insisted that Samuel report the oracle to him. Eli accepted the oracle of judgment on his house as the word of God and submitted to it.

The episode shows that Samuel had the capacity to experience visions from his youth. After this episode, the Lord was with Samuel and saw to it that his prophecies were not false (did not fall to the ground). Samuel succeeded Eli at a time when no genealogical successor was left in Eli's household. Now visions were no longer rare in the land, for the Lord continued to be revealed to Samuel at Shiloh.

SECOND LESSON: 1 CORINTHIANS 6:12-20

The problem here is that some Corinthian Christians were frequenting prostitutes, probably prostitutes for hire and not temple prostitutes, since the notion of idolatry does not appear. We learn from the passage the Corinthian rationale for such behavior and Paul's response.

The Corinthians believed that all ethical actions were permitted to them as Christians, based on two arguments. First, people had physical needs that should be met, which is expressed in the aphorism "The body was made for food and food for the body." The Corinthians extended this principle to include all physical desires and needs, including intercourse with prostitutes. Second, food and sexual intercourse had to do with the body only and did not affect the soul. God had saved the soul, and sin affected only the outward part of oneself and not the soul.

The Corinthians probably incorrectly inferred these principles from Paul's teaching. Paul taught that because of the death of Jesus, the Jewish law was now no longer in effect for Christians. Therefore they were now free, and all things were permissible for them. Paul may also have told them that food laws, indeed all ritual laws, made no difference one way or another for their salvation. They were free to eat or not eat (unless their eating harmed another person or was against their own conscience). Paul also may have argued that "sins" connected with eating affect the person outwardly but do not nullify the basic justification wrought by God on the cross. The Corinthians had misinterpreted Paul's meanings in all these matters, however, and had misapplied them to relations with prostitutes. In this section of the letter, Paul qualifies his teachings and corrects their misinterpretations.

In the first part (12-18a) Paul qualifies the Corinthian saying that "food was made for the stomach." Paul acknowledges that all things are lawful but adds that freedom is not good if it brings enslavement. He agrees that the stomach was made for food, but does not agree that the body was made for fornication. Although God will destroy food and stomach, God has made a claim upon the body—here meaning the whole person. Christ was raised and will raise up the whole person in the resurrection. So even now each person belongs to the corporate body of Christ. Thus a person is meant not for fornication but for the Lord. To reinforce this point, Paul adds that whoever is united to a prostitute becomes one body with her, a union incompatible with union to Christ/Spirit (not true of sexual union in marriage). Paul concludes with the exhortation "Avoid immorality!"

In the second part (18a-20) Paul qualifies the Corinthian slogan that "all sins committed are outside the body." He claims there is one exception. Fornication is against the body itself. Here Paul is thinking not only of the body of a person but also of the body of Christ as the community. Two arguments follow. First, Paul reminds the Corinthians that your (plural) body (i.e., the body of Christ) is the temple of the Holy Spirit. Therefore to violate the body of Christ is to violate the Holy Spirit, which dwells in the body of Christ. Second, Paul argues that the Corinthians are not their own, for they were bought with a price. Here Paul appeals to a slave market metaphor. Because you are bought and paid for, you already have a master and have no right to give yourself to another. This argument recalls the earlier caution not to be dominated by anything. God will be the only master, and God brings freedom. Paul ends with the exhortation "Glorify God in your body!"

GOSPEL: JOHN 1:35-51

Early in John's Gospel, an informal network of people tells news about Jesus. John the Baptist points out Jesus to two of his own disciples. Andrew was one of them, and he tells his brother Simon. Then Jesus comes into Galilee and calls Philip, who is from the same town as Andrew and Simon. Then Philip finds Nathanael, who in turn comes to see Jesus.

Each new member of the network has an understanding of who Jesus is. Each encounter reveals more about Jesus. John introduces Jesus as "the Lamb of God who takes away the sin of the world." Andrew tells Simon that they have found "the Messiah" (v. 41). Philip tells Nathanael that they have found "him about whom Moses in the law and also the prophets wrote." In turn, Nathanael responds to Jesus by saying, "You are the Son of God! You are the King of Israel!" Yet even these confessions are not adequate to the full meaning of Jesus. At the end of the episode, Jesus supercedes these Jewish titles and describes a universal Son of Humanity. As the one on whom the angels of heaven will ascend and descend, Jesus will be the site of God's glory to all people of the earth. John's subsequent narrative unfolds the full meaning of these revelations about Jesus.

When Philip says that Jesus is the one about whom Moses and the prophets "wrote," we realize that Philip and Nathanael are Jews who study Scripture. This impression is confirmed when Jesus sees Nathanael under a fig tree, for an Israelite under a fig tree symbolized an Israelite who studied Scripture. Jesus discerns in the heart of Nathanael an Israelite in whom there is no falseness. In John's Gospel it is precisely such a person— who knows Scripture and is without guile—who will understand who Jesus really is.

When Philip tells Nathanael that Jesus is from Nazareth of Galilee, he responds, "Can anything good come out of Nazareth?" Presumably Nathanael was surprised that the Messiah would have a lowly origin in a village in Galilee. In any case, Philip does not argue with Nathanael. Rather he invites him to "come and see." In the previous episode, John's disciples had asked Jesus, "Where are you staying?" Jesus had offered the same invitation to "come and see." As the story progresses, we readers realize that Jesus was really inviting them to "come and see" (discern) that Jesus is "staying" (abiding) in the Father. Similarly Philip's invitation to come and see is an invitation to discover that Jesus really comes not from Nazareth but from God.

HOMILETICAL REFLECTIONS

Epiphanies are manifestations of the extraordinary in the ordinary. An appearance of God is extraordinary. The extraordinary comes disguised in, embedded in, embodied in the ordinary: Samuel hears the Lord in a familiar voice; the glory of God is manifest in our bodies; a man from Nazareth is the definitive locus of the divine. The season of Epiphany continues the season of Christmas, because the incarnation is an epiphany of the extraordinary in the ordinary.

The presence of the extraordinary in the ordinary also describes the Eucharist as a locus of our encounter with God. Common staples like wine and bread bear the divine glory. The promise of Christ to be present in the Eucharist is not to imply that God is present nowhere else. On the contrary, if God is present in such ordinary elements as grape and grain, we can be sure God can be encountered anywhere.

The lesson from John is a window into the symbolism of the whole Gospel of John. For John the vehicles of the extraordinary are not only wine and bread, but water at a well, bread in a desert, vines and branches, gates of the sheepfold, light from the sun, shepherds, the temple in Jerusalem, the washing of feet; ordinary acts of "coming and seeing" all become concrete occasions to experience the reality of God. Today many experiences can be sacramental vehicles for an encounter with the divine— a birth, a brilliant rose, a symphony, an unexpected kindness, a sermon. Any of these can be an occasion for what Ian Ramsey (in *Religious Language* [London: SCM Press, 1957]) refers to as a "cosmic disclosure" of the nature of God. For Christians such epiphanies become rooted in and measured by the ultimate epiphany of the Christ event.

It might be appropriate to say here, even though the texts do not treat it directly, that this fitness for all things to bear God is also the key to an environmental theology. All things are potentially sacred and to be cared for with infinite kindness. If we treat creation like a throwaway, which can be left behind as humanity ascends to greater heights of progress or our souls fly off to heaven, then we will lose our own indispensable ecosystem. But if we see all the rich diversity of the good creation as a bearer of God's glory, then we will attend to creation in such a way that it (and we) will flourish. Such a profound incarnational understanding of nature weaves through Annie Dillard's books *Pilgrim at Tinker's Creek* (New

York: HarperCollins, 1988) and *Holy the Firm* (New York: Harper & Row, 1977). When we are pilgrims who experience the holy in the firmament at a creek, we pray truly to "dedicate ourselves to the care and redemption of all that you have made" (*LBW*, p. 68).

We can easily mistake and miss the extraordinary in the ordinary. God wears masks and is hidden even in the process of being revealed. No healings of Jesus were unambiguous signs. Those who did not have eyes to see did not see. Samuel thought Eli was calling him. The Corinthians thought the body could not bear the glory. Nathanael and Simon and Andrew saw the Son of God, while others saw a man possessed by the devil. As Jürgen Moltmann once commented, "If we do not expect the unexpected we will not see it." Sight and insight become important to experiencing traces of the divine. Clearly our modern scientific worldview tends to inhibit us from knowing invisible spiritual realities. Yet our modern worldview can be challenged and informed by the spiritual realities attested by the biblical worldview (see, for example, Marcus Borg, *Jesus: A New Vision* [San Francisco: Harper & Row, 1987]).

Another theme of our texts is that epiphanies make claims on people. We are impelled to be different, to respond. Epiphanies are voices that name us. Our response is as automatic as answering to our name. Paul claims that we belong to another, and our response is as natural as carrying out a social role. The men of Galilee saw Jesus and followed him. The claim made on us is not a legal requirement or a harping moral demand. Belonging to another is not a duty; it is a matter of being grasped by someone or something. The claim on us is a response intrinsic to the epiphany itself. Paul says, "You were washed, you were sanctified, you were justified," therefore . . . The response may be difficult: Samuel did not want to tell Eli, and Jesus' disciples struggled mightily as they followed. But the response issues from the encounter.

A friend of mine once described an extraordinary near-death encounter with light, which he understood to be Jesus. Without a trace of judgment, Jesus addressed him: "What have you done with your life?" This encounter resulted in a dramatic transformation of his life. Others see light at more ordinary moments in a sudden recognition of grace or of love behind the surface of things or of the "dearest freshness deep down things" (G. M. Hopkins)—and they are no longer the same. Few people today will follow the Christian life just because the Bible says so. We are called therefore to articulate the biblical story so persuasively and transparently that an experience of the presence of God, some epiphany, will grasp people and make claims on them. Then they will follow.

God wills nothing less than to transform and glorify our whole selves. God wills for our work, our relationships with friends and enemies, our families, our sexual life, our use of money, our church communities to manifest the glory of God. To Paul a human being is not divided into soul and body. God has made a claim on the whole self along with all our ethical responsibilities. Any claim that religion (Christianity) has only to do with the soul and nothing to do with sex, politics, or business is not biblical. In Paul's view we have not been saved by Christ *from* creation. Rather we have been redeemed to be our true selves *in* and *for* the world. This is incarnational theology. Therefore glorify God in your body.

Concrete ethical actions issue from the nature of the glory revealed in the epiphany. Paul translates his incredible experience of grace into guidelines for relationships in community. To remain in the new reality of grace, followers act in ways consistent with grace. We treat others with the same love that God expressed in justifying us in Christ. We shape our holy actions by the Holy Spirit. Therefore glorify God in your (plural) body (of Christ).

Thus the claims God makes on us are moral but not moralistic, responsible but not legalistic. To relate biblical ethics to the twentieth century is not a matter of obeying biblical rules and commands. It is to experience grace, to have our character shaped by the Spirit, and then to make informed decisions of courage about what God wills for our particular time and circumstance.

Finally, evangelism rooted in epiphany is not legalistic. We cannot force or manipulate anyone to experience an epiphany. Instead, we invite others to "come and see." We invite people into our community, into our sphere of language and insight, into our worship, into the orbit of grace, into our lives—in the hope that they might see Jesus and recognize that he abides in God. Then they too might abide in God.

Third Sunday after the Epiphany

Lutheran	Roman Catholic	Episcopal	Common Lectionary
Jon. 3:1-5, 10	Jon. 3:1-5, 10	Jer. 3:21—4:2	Jon. 3:1-5, 10
1 Cor. 7:29-31	1 Cor. 7:29-31	1 Cor. 7:17-23	1 Cor. 7:29-31 (32-35)
Mark 1:14-20	Mark 1:14-20	Mark 1:14-20	Mark 1:14-20

FIRST LESSON: JONAH 3:1-10

The scenario for this delightful story is that God's calling of a Jewish prophet to warn the wicked capital of the Babylonian Empire, which had conquered Israel and dragged its people into captivity. Jonah wants this cruel foreign city to get what it has coming to it with no warnings and no mercy. He fears that Nineveh might repent and God relent. So he takes a ship in the opposite direction.

But God gives Jonah a second chance and has him thrown from the ship, swallowed by a big fish, and spit up on shore toward Nineveh. Jonah will do his duty, but he will also try to thwart success. He travels only one day into a city three days' journey across. He never gets to the center of the city, so most people hear his prophecy indirectly. He does not identify the offending sins or call for repentance. He speaks five words in Hebrew announcing the impending doom: "Forty days—Nineveh will perish." He tries to be as ineffectual as possible.

The king believes immediately and declares a total fast, commanding everyone—even the animals—to wear sackcloth. He calls everyone to repent of their violent ways. Then he sits in the dust to see what will happen. The hated enemies of Israel are a model of repentance: they hear God despite the offensiveness of the prophecy; they acknowledge God's judgment and repent of their sin; they know that God is sovereign and that their repentance cannot guarantee in some magical way the removal of the threat (3:9); and their king acts in the best interests of the people. In turn, God repents of destroying Nineveh. Meanwhile Jonah, knowing his worst fears will be realized, waits on a hill outside Nineveh to see what will happen. He would rather die than have God show mercy to these wicked people.

The story is rife with satire meant to reveal the readers to themselves: God is God of all the world and not just Israel; God cares about other nations as much as Israel; Israel should want others to have God's mercy as they have; God is merciful and will repent in response to repentance; Israel should repent as the Ninevites did; and much more. The story subverts the readers' claim to privilege and teaches us to love the enemy.

SECOND LESSON: 1 CORINTHIANS 7:29-31

In this section of the letter dealing with sexual relations (7:1-40), Paul writes that sexual relations in marriage are good but that it is best to remain unmarried.

The Corinthian Christians were blessed (and confused) by a cornucopia of spiritual gifts—so much so that they believed they had already arrived, already transcended the flesh, and were reigning in the kingdom of God. Reflecting the body—soul dualism of Greek thought, the Corinthians sep-- arated spirit (both the Holy Spirit and their own spirit/soul) from life in the flesh. Some concluded that spirit alone was important and that it did not matter what they did in the flesh; these libertine Christians united with prostitutes. Others believed that since they were now living in the Spirit, they should deny all the needs and desires of the flesh; these ascetic Christians believed that it was better for a man not to touch a woman even in marriage.

In the passage preceding this one, Paul had said that Christians should remain as they were when they were converted. If married, stay married—unless an unbelieving spouse wants to separate. If unmarried, stay un-married—but if one has difficulty with sexual drives, get married rather than burn with lust or commit fornication. Here is the traditional Jewish view of the goodness of marriage. Each man should have his own wife, each wife her own husband. Marital responsibilities should be taken se-riously. Paul adds that one may divorce an unbelieving spouse and that remarriage after divorce (not after a spouse's death) is prohibited. Paul also says not to get married unless necessary.

Paul advocated remaining unmarried for two reasons, both due to the "present crisis" of an impending end. First, Paul believed that people were living in the last days and that the resurrection of Jesus was the first fruits of a general resurrection soon to follow. This world was passing away and there would soon be a new transformed reality. Although people still had responsibilities, they were to do them as participants of the coming age rather than as part of the old age. As such, marriage for procreation made no sense, because neither marriage nor the begetting of children would be part of the new age. It would not be wise to get too attached to the present age—in marriage or in buying and selling or in rejoicing and mourning.

Paul's second reason for urging Christians to remain unmarried was his belief that the "present crisis" required great loyalty to the Lord. This was the time of the messianic woes, the trials and tribulations of the last days, with rejection, recrimination, and persecution for Christians. Paul himself had undergone trials, beatings, and imprisonments. He might not have taken such risks for the Lord had he also been responsible to a spouse. Therefore it would be better for people to remain unmarried "as I am."

Paul thought that marriage would create divided loyalties between the affairs of the Lord and the cares and anxieties of marriage, between pleasing the Lord and pleasing the spouse. Better to invest in the new age than the old age. Better to invest in the affairs of the Lord than the affairs of the world. Better to remain unmarried, even though it is not wrong to marry in the Lord. An unmarried state would promote good order, freedom from worldly anxiety, and unhindered devotion to the Lord.

A word of caution. Because Paul expected the world to end soon, he told people to remain as slaves if they were slaves and not to marry if they were unmarried. He sought to create a new social order *within* the Christian community without changing the world around him—for the world was passing away. We, by contrast, are living in a situation very different from Paul's. We hope the world will not pass away but will be transformed. Our ethical choices are therefore different from those of Paul's time. We promote Christian humane values not only in the church but also in society beyond the boundaries of the Christian community.

GOSPEL: MARK 1:14-20

Jesus announces God's kingdom. The first part of the announcement declares good news about God: "The time is fulfilled, the rule of God has arrived." This announcement follows Jesus' successful encounter with Satan in the desert. Satan will no longer be in charge, for God's power is now available to overcome all obstacles to full humanity. The subsequent narrative is commentary on this announcement, for the Gospel is the display of the kingdom.

The second part of Jesus' announcement calls for a response to the kingdom: "Repent, and believe in the good news." Repentance is a reorienting of the self or the community. In John's baptism, one turned *from* past sins to be forgiven. With Jesus' announcement, one turns *toward* the new reality of the kingdom of God. Faith is the proper reception of the kingdom. Faith grants access to the power of the kingdom for healing and service.

The next episode in the pericope is an enactment of the announcement. Jesus says: "Follow me and I will make you fish for people." Jesus calls fishermen from their work by the sea to join him in inaugurating God's rule, two pairs of brothers working together in a family cooperative in the village of Capernaum. They respond with faith. They understand Jesus to be calling them to discipleship, and they drop everything to follow. As Galileans, they had not participated in John's baptism with Judeans and the Jerusalemites. They do not know that Jesus is the Messiah. Yet Jesus calls them, and they follow. They follow not really knowing where the teacher will take them or what the cost will be. They find out as they go.

Their finding out as they go is a quest for faith. In Mark faith is trusting in the reign of God. It involves a letting go of the things we cling to for security and identity—possessions, family, power, status, financial security, or life itself. Such relinquishing takes faith in God. Faith that one's future well-being is in God's hand grants the courage to live for God in the present despite the cost. The disciples had to break with the relationships that kept them stationary so that they could go from place to place to fish for people. In the course of following Jesus, they also broke with the values of society and adopted the values of the kingdom. They relinquished their story to adopt God's story as their own.

It is also interesting to note the temporal and spatial dimensions of the kingdom. In Mark's understanding, time is not chronological but opportune time. Kingdom time is ripe time, time come to fullness and fulfillment. This time has a dimension of urgency, because the opportunity for repentance will last only so long (the word *immediately* is used repeatedly). God's time is not our time, and opportunities that present themselves do not come again. We see the spatial dimension of the kingdom from the beginning. Jesus and the disciples are "on the way," going from village to village bringing the power of the kingdom throughout Israel. Eventually they will spread the kingdom to all the Gentile nations. The temporal dimension of the kingdom correlates with the spatial dimension: Before the time is up for the rule of God to be fully established, followers are to proclaim the kingdom to all the earth.

HOMILETICAL REFLECTIONS

In these lessons we see the relationship between God's story and our stories. God had a story for Babylon but it did not suit Jonah's scenario. God called the Corinthians into community, but each faction promoted its own agenda. Jesus announced the kingdom and the disciples responded immediately, although they had difficulty later in letting go of their own hopes for power and glory. The call to disipleship is the call to adopt God's story as our story.

Epiphany comes as a revelation of God's purposes. The kingdom is God's story for the world. We can read the whole Gospel (indeed the whole Bible) to see the full dimensions of this work. There is hope for healing, power over evil, an acceptance of outcasts, liberation from oppression, empowerment for service, and spiritual resources for community. God is at work in the world, and the ministry of Jesus reveals the nature of that work. Concrete expressions, in particular human circumstances, change from era to era and culture to culture, but the basic features of God's work remain the same.

Epiphany comes in the form of a call to live for the reign of God on earth. God's story/reign has temporal dimensions—opportunities to repent and do God's work. The reign of God has spatial dimensions—making the familial, commercial, political, and economic arenas of our lives into expressions of God's reign. We see both the temporal and spatial dimensions in the ecological crisis. God's story is the "redemption of all that God has made." We are called to redeem the time, to repent now of our devastation of the earth. The changes required at personal and corporate levels are staggering. Yet if we do not act, countless generations will suffer. We are called to redeem the earth as space where God reigns. Then we will care for the earth and sustain life. We can learn much from the Bible about how to respond to sacred time—by breaking with society's values, by repenting, by acting unilaterally. In turn, we can learn much, for example, from Native American Christians about how to live in sacred space—the earth is God's, every creature is sacred, and we share nature as a common responsibility (See Vine Deloria, *God is Red* [New York: Grosset & Dunlap, 1963]).

As such, these episodes are about vocation: Jonah's vocation to declare God's reprieve for Babylon, the Corinthians' vocation to be Christians in community, the disciples' vocation to follow Jesus in faith. Our culture provides us with many compelling stories to emulate. But the issue for Christian vocation is, What is God's story? A hospital chaplain in Kansas once explained his view of ministry. He left his own agenda at the door of each room and asked this question: What is God already doing in this person's life, and how can I cooperate? We can ask: What is God doing in the world, and how can we be agents for that work? This is not to say that God has some detailed plan laid out for our lives; but God does have an open story that we are called to join.

Lutheran theologian Joseph Sittler once said that there is really only one vocation—the human vocation. To follow Jesus is a quest to be human in the highest sense. Our jobs, careers, family commitments, friendships, and so on are particular facets of our larger human vocation. Our commitment to God is not a loyalty that lies alongside other loyalties, and it is not to be equated with church responsibilities. The human vocation given us by God shapes and undergirds all we do. For this task we Christians need ongoing vocational training.

The Christian/human vocation involves both an investment in the things of our lives and a detachment from them. We carry out many roles in life, but our ultimate meaning and purpose transcend them. We vote, but we vote in the interests of all rather than merely for self. We make commitments to others, but our resources for fidelity are deeper than the appeal or commitment of the other. We love our country, but we support a national policy built on the well-being of all nations. We barber or work in a pet store or make cars or try cases in court or teach or nurse or parent or whatever, and all these are shaped by our participation in God's story.

Sometimes our larger human vocation conflicts with the way we carry out our particular commitments. Homiletician Morris Niedenthal was preaching in his church in Kansas on the theme of being little Christs to our neighbors. After worship a man came up and said that based on the sermon he had decided to quit his job. He sold vacuum cleaners, and at the sales meeting every Saturday, the manager told them their one purpose was to destroy the competition. The decision was no small matter, because the man was married with seven children and this was his only income. What a dilemma! Our commitment to God may clash with the responsibilities of a job or with the demands a friend makes on us. It may clash with our national obligations: a conscientious objector who will not inflict death or a civil protestor who disobeys unjust laws.

The ultimate test of our adherence to God's story comes in our attitude toward our enemies, both personal and national enemies. Like Jonah, we tend to see the enemy as evil and ourselves as good, the enemy as less than human and ourselves as humane. The enemy is "the other." And since enemies are beyond redemption, we have every right to crush them mercilessly. Like Jonah, we want to destroy them without remorse. Such an attitude polarizes people and eclipses reconciliation.

But God's story is larger than our story. God is creator of all people and desires to redeem all. All have sinned and fallen short of God's glory, and all have been justified by God's mercy. Hard decisions are necessary, but *how* they are made is crucial. Lincoln was once told with relish that three hundred confederate soldiers had perished in battle, whereupon Lincoln wept. The bearer of the news wondered why, since they were the enemy. Lincoln replied, "Sir, you have a very small heart." We are called to have a heart as large as God's heart, to live God's story as our vocation in the kingdom.

The good news of epiphany is that God is enacting a liberating story for this world. God has called us, chosen us, and commissioned us to the high purpose of God's work in the world. Our vocation is to let God weave God's story through us.

Fourth Sunday after the Epiphany

Lutheran	Roman Catholic	Episcopal	Common Lectionary
Deut. 18:15-20	Deut. 18:15-20	Deut. 18:15-30	Deut. 18:15-20
1 Cor. 8:1-13	1 Cor. 7:32-35	1 Cor. 8:1b-13	1 Cor. 8:1-13
Mark 1:21-28	Mark 1:21-28	Mark 1:21-28	Mark 1:21-28

FIRST LESSON: DEUTERONOMY 18:15-20

Deuteronomy 18 lists illegal forms of divination and defines true and false prophets. Prohibited are casting lots, discerning from dregs in a cup, divining with arrows, and seeking out spirits of the dead. These practices infringe on God's rule over creation. Unlike other nations, the Israelites have no need to stir up action from an impassive god or to control the unpredictable actions of a whimsical god. Israel's God will take the initiative and will govern the world through prophets.

God will raise up prophets like Moses. This statement, in itself prophetic, refers to prophets who will appear as God needs them. From time to time God will raise up a prophet like Moses to speak the word of the Lord to the people. God used prophets as intermediaries, because the people feared they would die if God addressed them directly. God will rule through the prophets by words. God had created the world through words in the first place. God will continue the creative governance of the world through powerful words of prophecy and command. The people ignore these words at their peril.

Like Moses, the prophets will be teachers and compassionate intercessors obedient to God. False prophets speak when they have no message from God or speak in the name of another god. The verification of true prophecy suggested by Deuteronomy will be difficult, because one will not know if the prophecy is true until the event happens. That may be too late for the people to decide whether the prophet should be heeded.

SECOND LESSON: 1 CORINTHIANS 8:1-13

This is the first of four parts in this letter dealing with Christian freedom. Here Paul deals with eating meat offered to idols (see also 10:1—11:1).

In Corinth, as throughout the empire, idols were everywhere. Most meat was slaughtered in the local temples and parts of the animal were offered to the gods. The rest was made available to the public—at festivals or in public dining areas of a temple or at private parties (e.g., a marriage) or for consumption in private homes. In principle Paul had no objection to eating meat on any of these occasions as long as one did not participate in the actual cultic meal to the god (10:20).

The Corinthian Christians were divided. Some did not believe idols existed and ate meat offered to idols without pangs of conscience. Paul refers to this group as the strong. Others believed the idols were gods, and it troubled their conscience to eat meat sacrificed to idols. These may have included Gentile Christians with previous experience in idol worship or Jewish Christians who as Jews had never eaten meat sacrificed to idols and could not exercise their freedom as Christians to do it now. Paul refers to this group as the weak.

In *The Social Setting of Pauline Christianity*, Gerd Theissen argues that the strong group may have been wealthy Christians who could afford meat, who were leaders in the community and thus needed the social contact with pagans. The weak were probably the low-born, uneducated, and poor of the community who did not eat meat often and for whom the experience of eating meat was probably strange. The weak were offended by the strong or tempted to go along with them. In so doing they were going against their conscience and jeopardizing their relation with God.

Paul's response in this section of the letter is organized around three sayings of the Corinthians with which Paul agrees but which he qualifies. Note how Paul encourages the unity of the church by giving basic agreement with the strong but then qualifying their point of view out of consideration for the weak.

First, Paul agrees with the strong that "all [Christians] have knowledge." He qualifies it, however, by asserting that "knowledge puffs up." Paul is not against knowledge in and of itself—either spiritual or mundane knowledge. Rather he is against the use of knowledge apart from love. Without love, knowledge leads to arrogance in relation to others who do not have the same knowledge. This yields no benefit to others and results in division in the community. True knowledge is rooted in love, and love is rooted in being known by God. In this way Paul distinguishes knowledge of God from idolatry. You may know an idol but it does not know you. But God knows you, has chosen you, and loves you. That is the root of the knowledge that does not puff up.

Second, Paul agrees that "no idol exists." Although there are so-called gods and lords (created things people call gods), there is only one God and one Lord who is the source of creation and through whom we have life. Here is the God who created all, redeems all, and gives unity to all. Yet, Paul adds, not everyone has the knowledge that idols are not gods, such as the weak whose conscience would be defiled if they ate. Paul does not agree with the weak, but he has utmost respect for their conscience.

Finally, Paul agrees that "food will not bring us close to God." Paul has announced that "all things are lawful," and Christians are free not to engage in any food restrictions whatsoever. Food does not commend one to God (Romans 14). Paul does not consider such freedom, however, to be license to disregard others. Here he shifts to the second person and addresses the strong directly: "Take care that your freedom does not become a stumbling block to the weak." If the strong mislead the weak into eating meat offered to idols, they may destroy them by obviating their salvation. This sin of the strong is compounded: To destroy a brother or sister is to sin against (the body of) Christ. Paul claims he would never use his freedom to cause someone else's fall.

GOSPEL: MARK 1:21-28

Here is an astounding story showing Jesus' power as agent of the reign of God. Jesus enters an official institution, the synagogue, where the common people contrast his authority with that of the scribes of the law. As the story unfolds, it becomes clear how Jesus "teaches with authority": He exorcises, heals illnesses, pardons sins, interprets the law with actions, and teaches in parables.

The exorcism demonstrates Jesus' power and authority. The unclean spirit knows Jesus. In his terror, the demon reveals that Jesus came to destroy the unclean spirits, and in an effort to control Jesus, the demon names him "the Holy One of God." Jesus rebukes the unclean spirit, saying, " 'Be silent, and come out of him.' " This is a two-part response (in inverse order) to the two statements of the demon. After the demon calls him the Holy One of God, Jesus tells it to be quiet (the first instance of the so-called messianic secret). After the demon asks whether Jesus has come to destroy it, Jesus effectively destroys the demon, saying, " 'Come out of him,' " and the unclean spirit shakes the man, screams, and comes out. Jesus' words are actions, like God's words. They effect what they speak. The crowd is appropriately amazed, saying, " 'What is this? A new teaching—with authority! He commands even the unclean spirits, and they obey him.' "

This story contains several interesting features. First, the conflict between Jesus and the demon is loud and violent. It is a conflict between ultimate forms of power: Jesus has a (the) Holy Spirit and the demoniac has an unclean spirit, Jesus acts for God and the demon acts for Satan. It is clear that the kingdom of God has indeed arrived, for Jesus has little difficulty destroying the unclean spirit. This conflict is a local skirmish in the cosmic struggle over power and territory. Note too that the possessed man plays a passive role. While the sick come in faith, demoniacs are incapable of faith. Demoniacs are either brought to Jesus by others who have faith for them or the demons confront Jesus directly. Finally, it is interesting to note that the Markan unclean spirits have the same traits as the evil people in the story, but to an extreme: They dominate people, are terrified of losing their lives, and seek to destroy those who threaten their existence.

It is not obvious from this passage, but it is important to note, that Jesus' authority has limits. In Mark, Jesus wields authority over demons, illnesses (when people have faith), and natural forces (seas, deserts, trees)—nonhuman forces that oppress people. Jesus wields no authority, however, over people. He cannot heal people without faith, make them keep quiet if they wish to speak, or force his disciples to understand his teachings. Jesus is the true human as God created humans, with authority (dominion) over all aspects of life but no authority to lord over other human beings. Jesus has divine authority to serve people, whereas the scribes have human authority and lord over people. The whole Gospel unpacks the contrast between these two notions of authority.

HOMILETICAL REFLECTIONS

These lessons deal with the use and misuse of God's power and of human power. Epiphanies are the manifestation of God as power. Because the power of God's presence was so terrifying, the Israelites insisted that God address them through mediators. Corinthians knew the gods in terms of power, and some feared the consequences of eating meat offered to idols. Jesus' confrontation in the synagogue was a conflict of naked power in which the Holy Spirit overcame the power of evil spirits. In *The Idea of the Holy* (Oxford: Oxford Univ. Press, 1950), Rudolf Otto presents a more recent articulation of God's power as the *mysterium tremendum*—holy power.

Although not central to mainline Christianity in North America, the manifestation of God's power is crucial in many parts of the world to overcome the evil powers involved in possession, devil worship, sorcery, and witchcraft, as well as the misuse of God's power through divination. Appropriate expressions of God's power to overcome evil through exorcism and prayer are consistent with the biblical witness. The question is not whether there is power but what kind of power and how it is used.

The Bible portrays God's power as borne by words. In the Hebrew culture, words were actions. God said, "Let there be light, and there was light." Isaac blessed Jacob instead of Esau, and he could not take it back. In the lesson from Deuteronomy, God promises to rule by putting divine words in the mouths of the prophets. Later the prophets "told forth" the future, and the events were to come true because the prophets spoke the words as God's words. In Mark's account Jesus exercised power in words. He told the demon to get out, and the demon went. He told the leper, "Be cleansed," and he was healed.

Today we tend to think of words primarily as designations of meaning. Yet words clearly have power. The pastor says, for example, "I now pronounce you husband and wife" or "I declare the entire forgiveness of all your sins." These are actions that have effects. In fact language always "does" something. In *How to do Things with Words* (Cambridge: Harvard Univ. Press, 1962), John Austin argues that all words have a "performative" function. When we speak, we judge or inform or persuade or correct or soothe or affirm and so on. Thus our words can serve God's reign; they can liberate, heal, forgive, bless, or respect. Conversely we can destroy, strike fear, belittle, or dismiss with our words. We count on God's investment for salvation in the words we acclaim in preaching and in sacraments. We are called to trust that God will be active through our words to bring wholeness and healing. We are called as Christians to use words in the service of God's power.

In Corinthians the issue is the misuse of God's power and human power. The strong in Corinth have no right to exercise their spiritual rights if it harms another in the community. Love is the constraint on the misuse of power. We should use our power to build up people in the various social communities of which we are a part and not to threaten or subvert them.

In 1 Corinthians Paul's understanding of power is rooted in his theology of the cross. God worked through Jesus by a free choice on Jesus' part not to use coercive power. The power of the cross was the refusal to use power, the willingness to choose weakness rather than to seek revenge or to destroy. The power of weakness was the power of salvation, because it empowered people to live so as to build others up rather than tear them down, to look out for the interests of others rather than one's own, to foster harmony rather than create division. The result is a theology of mutuality in which all exercise their gifts from God to provide wholeness for individuals within a healthy community. This is the kind of empowerment that continues the new world God created through the cross.

The freedom to exercise power does not grant the moral right to use it. Freedom is not freedom if it is license to disregard others. As humans we rightly cherish freedom. The result, however, has sometimes been that we feel we have a moral right to exercise our freedom or power even when it destroys others. We assume people have the right to accumulate as much wealth as they can. Executives of companies and major stockholders sometimes have outrageously high incomes, while workers are paid little and prices are high. As long as people are oppressed or hungry or poor, the personal accumulation of wealth by some will be at the expense of or at the neglect of others. How can we limit wealth and use wealth out of God's vision for all humanity, distributing it equitably to build people up rather than tear them down? Paul's letters offer no blueprints for the complex issues of our time. But we are invited to assimilate the theology of the cross, the ethic of mutuality, and then to see in what creative ways we can be faithful.

Mark believes all power should be used in service. Jesus has power over demons, illness, and nature, but not over humans. He sees servants and slaves as models for the use of power. Everything a servant does is for the benefit of others. Servants do not have anyone under them as a means of self-aggrandizement. Mark argues that all power should be used for service.

We need to be certain that talk of service does not reinforce social roles in which service is constrained and not freely chosen. To use Mark's theology of service in order to perpetuate subordinate roles for women and blacks, for example, is exactly opposite to biblical intentions. Mark's entire approach is to overcome human oppression and exploitation. Jesus was executed because he opposed oppression. As such, the message of service in Mark and in Paul is directed especially to those who are called to give up power and authority. Free males were called to relinquish social privilege and place in order to effect a relationship of equity and mutuality. Conversely women, slaves, and the low-born who have been denied rights and freedoms were called to exercise those rights in order to attain mutuality.

When people have epiphanies, they sometimes interpret their experience as granting a right to force their beliefs or experiences on others. Our lessons show that God's power is manifest to serve and bring life, never to oppress.

Fifth Sunday after the Epiphany

Lutheran	Roman Catholic	Episcopal	Common Lectionary
Job 7:1-7	Job 7:1-4, 6-7	2 Kings 4:18-21, 32-37	Job 7:1-7
1 Cor. 9:16-23	1 Cor. 9:16-19, 22-23	1 Cor. 9:16-23	1 Cor. 9:16-23
Mark 1:29-39	Mark 1:29-39	Mark 1:29-39	Mark 1:29-39

FIRST LESSON: JOB 7:1-7

Satan was the prosecuting attorney in the heavenly council. God had given Satan leeway to test Job to see if he would be faithful or curse God (1:1—2:13). Job did not know why he was suffering and he took his case before God. Those who came to "comfort" Job (Eliphaz, Bildad, and Zophar) argued that God is just and therefore Job must be at fault or he would not have been suffering. Job knew that the comforters were not right. He was suffering unjustly. This passage, Job's response to Eliphaz, offers his complaint about the miseries of life.

Life is hard labor; indeed it is like slave labor for God. Slaves are in such misery that they long for the grave. Laborers are paid from day to day, and their bare subsistence depends on getting wages daily. But they work in the heat of the day and then have their wages held back. It is a miserable existence. It is also an empty life. You worry about when to rise even before you lie down. The nights are long and restless. In the life of poverty, the body is covered with worms and dirt, the skin hardens and then breaks out in blisters. Life goes by quickly and runs out of hope. Because life depends on breath, we will die and never see God again.

Make your own catalog of the miseries of those who today live on the edge of life and death. There are no answers to this misery. Even the epiphany that Job received at the end of the story was not an "answer." Rather it was an overwhelming experience of the greatness of God, an experience that did not explain his condition but that nevertheless enabled Job to entrust himself to God.

SECOND LESSON: 1 CORINTHIANS 9:16-23

Again we see the main issue of the entire letter: How can the Corinthian Christians avoid dissension and division? Paul has been explaining to the strong that they need to curtail their rights so as not to cause weaker members to go against their own consciences. In chapter 9, Paul gives an extended example of the way he himself has relinquished his own rights for the sake of others. He ends by encouraging the Corinthians to imitate him, as he imitates the Lord.

As an apostle, Paul has a right to food, marriage, and support for life. He bases this right on a number of arguments: the practices of other apostles, the customs of other occupations, such as soldiering, a citation from the law about not muzzling the ox, cultic practices, and a command from the Lord. But Paul says he would rather die than exercise these apostolic rights. Let no one, he says, take away his grounds for boasting. Immediately, however, he clarifies this. His boasting is not in his preaching of the gospel, for then he would "deserve" the rights he might exercise. He preaches because he is under necessity, for a responsibility has been laid on him that he cannot ignore. He has no choice about it.

Yet Paul does have a choice about how he will carry out the obligation. He can do it with resentment, seeking to get as much as possible from his rights, or he can show his "choice" of the obligation by forgoing his rights as an apostle and preaching free of charge. Even Paul's boast about preaching the gospel free of charge is not rooted in Paul's own achievement; rather it is a response to the privilege and joy of the necessity that has been laid on him. Paul does not deny the freedom of others to exercise their rights as apostles, but he does not want anyone to take his choice away.

Now Paul goes further and tells what else he gives up for the gospel. He is free with respect to all people; others place no necessity of action on him. But Paul has willingly made himself slave of all in order to win some. He becomes as one under the law (a Jew) or as one outside the law (a Gentile) or as one who is weak. He becomes all things to all people in order to save some. This may sound opportunistic. But Paul does not do it for himself, for his behavior is actually a denial of his own rights on behalf of others. Nor does he do it to please others, for the cross he preaches is a scandal to Jews and foolishness to Greeks. Nor does he do it out of fear of offending others or being rejected, for he endures much persecution. Neither does he do it as mere accommodation and compromise, for he is committed to the gospel. No, he gives up his right and freedom in Christ out of solidarity with those for whom Christ died in the hope that they may be saved. Therefore those who have been saved through him, the Corinthians themselves, are Paul's boast.

It may seem that being all things to all people will lead Paul to relinquish his integrity. But Paul does not think one is saved by law, so he can be as one under the law. He does not think one is saved by being outside the law, so he can be as such. He does not think that the traditions of the weak (refusing to eat meat offered to idols at Corinth) will commend or not commend one to God, so he is free to eat or not eat. Paul reasons that it is not right for people to insist on acting according to their integrity without taking account of the effects on others; that is, integrity apart from love leads to arrogance and self-righteousness (see Krister Stendahl, *Paul among Jews and Gentiles* [Philadelphia: Fortress Press, 1976]). Paul has only one guide to his actions. He is in the "law of Christ," that is, he "loves the neighbor as oneself." For Paul this is not another set of external obligations. It is an orbit of grace into which Paul has been drawn, and Paul seeks to act in consonance with this sphere of grace.

Thus, Paul does not see his willingness to be all things to all people as a violation either of himself or of others. On the contrary, he sees it as an expression of the theology of the cross so central to this letter. The death of Jesus on the cross expresses the willingness to relinquish one's self, one's power, one's wisdom, and one's life on behalf of others. Thus, the Christian is free, but freedom itself is not absolute. The Christian (like the apostle) has rights, but the exercise of one's rights is not an absolute. A Christian has integrity, but even one's personal integrity for its own sake is not an absolute. Rather love is the source and guide, love exercised in the greatest concern for the other. Love is not one among many virtues, not the highest of duties. It is the way all things can be done. Without it neither sacrifice nor faith nor hope has substance. This love makes unity possible amid diversity of belief, practice, and ethic. Jesus showed this love in the cross. Paul shows this love when he relinquishes his rights for the benefit of others. In turn, Paul encourages the Corinthians to imitate him, as he imitates Jesus, so that they may avoid quarrels and divisions.

GOSPEL: MARK 1:29-39

After exorcising a demon in the synagogue, Jesus heals Peter's mother-in-law. The healing thus takes place on the Sabbath, which is against the Jewish law. Jesus' reputation as exorcist and healer spreads quickly. As soon as the Sabbath passes ("evening, at sundown"), the whole city gathers with their sick and possessed. Early in the morning Jesus goes to the desert, an episode that recalls his earlier testing. Here Jesus is reorienting himself to God's will in prayer. He is determined to proclaim to other villages, because "that is what I came out to do."

Simon's mother-in-law is the first of many people who come to Jesus or who are brought to Jesus by supplicants. The disciples tell Jesus about her. Jesus goes to her, grasps her hand, and raises her up. Then, Mark says, "the fever left her, and she began to serve them." Mark's concern here is not simply with the illness but with the results of the illness—her inability to serve others. The restoration to health is accompanied by a restoration of her relationships with people. Elsewhere Jesus is likewise concerned with reversing the isolation of the leper, restoring family relationships to the demoniac, and enabling the blind man to go on his way. In the Gospels, Jesus' concerns about bodily healing include a desire to restore quality of life and community to the person.

Here too we see Jesus' initial conflict with the disciples. The disciples are enamored of the crowds at Capernaum and surprised that Jesus is off in a deserted place. By contrast, Jesus is not enamored of the crowd. He does not seek to build a reputation. Jesus does not get his authority from humans. He gets his authority and direction from God, and therefore he is here praying. His purpose is to " 'go on to the neighboring towns, so that I may proclaim the message there also.' " The mandate of the kingdom drives Jesus, not the acclamation of the crowds. Mark weaves this conflict of values between Jesus and the disciples throughout his entire story.

HOMILETICAL REFLECTIONS

Human suffering is a common thread in these lessons. Job poignantly articulates the unrelieved hardships of a peasant life worn down by subsistence living. Paul deals with the pain that results from the absence of love in human relationships. Mark depicts Jesus ministering to those who were below subsistence level because of their illness, uncleanness, or disability. Here epiphany is the manifestation of God in the restoration of wholeness.

The epiphany, or work, of God in the world is the relief of human suffering. In the Bible salvation involves deliverance from all kinds of human conflict and misfortune. Paul seeks to bring reconciliation to broken communities. Jesus drives out demons, heals the sick, rescues people from the threats of nature, commands people to give to the poor, condemns oppression, and liberates people from the destructiveness of their own sins. The healing of human brokenness is an adequate comprehensive depiction of the saving, healing, reconciling ministry of the church. Christianity is a healing ministry that brings wholeness to persons in healthy communities.

The problem with illness and other tragic suffering is that they often persist despite our prayers. This is Job's agony, the absence of a restoring epiphany. In the season of Epiphany, we need to face squarely the problem that epiphanies do not come. It does no good to be relentlessly optimistic about healing without dealing realistically with the problem of ongoing suffering. The sick are not served by people who tell them that if they just thought more positively they would be healed. The sick are not served by those who claim that the absence of healing must be God's will. Telling people they do not have enough faith only induces guilt and more pain. That is to be like Job's comforters, who defend God (and blame people) when defending God is destructive.

It is simply a fact that people with great faith in God often are not healed. This does not mean we avoid praying because of fear of failure or disappointment. Rather we can pray with trust in God, without undercutting our hope for healing and without making the prayer a test of God. Sometimes people are healed in ways we could only describe as miraculous. Sometimes people are renewed by prayer and loving companionship. Sometimes, like Job, people are renewed by God even when they do not recover from the illness (see Arthur Frank, *At the Will of the Body: Reflections on Illness* [Boston: Houghton Mifflin, 1991]).

People frequently misunderstand suffering. Suffering does not come as a punishment from God for sin. Suffering is not connected to our worth, and we do not deserve it. Jesus healed all who came to him desiring it, and he did it with no strings attached. Healing is a gift, and it is not connected to our worth any more than suffering is. The Gospels show that God clearly wants wholeness for people and relief from illness and suffering. Still we are left with this question: If God is loving and powerful, why is there suffering? The Christian tradition has resources to offer this issue but no resolutions which eliminate the tragedy of human suffering. We trust in the goodness of God even when we do not understand why there is so much suffering.

Christians have many opportunities to engage in the healing ministry of the kingdom. Many jobs and vocations are oriented directly or indirectly toward the easing of human suffering. If we can see the work we already do as a ministry of service to those in need, we can seek to carry out that work in ways worthy of the kingdom. Others voluntarily work for those in need. Many Christians in our congregations and neighborhoods are "natural care givers" who look in on a sick neighbor or give food to a homeless person or relieve someone who gives long-term care to a relative. Some become involved with local service organizations—as donors, members of boards, volunteers in shelters for the homeless, advocates for a safe environment, or relief workers in national disaster areas. Like Paul, we are called to suffer the sacrifices of love in the service of relieving suffering.

As communities of caring, congregations can nurture the healing ministry. The church can foster and train those who have special gifts of healing. The church can help all of us see the healing dimensions in our daily work. It can promote our involvement in volunteer forms of ministry outside church structures and provide opportunities from within church structures to heal in communities and neighborhoods. The church can celebrate healing and reconciliation wherever they take place in God's world—

hospitals, negotiating tables, services for the poor. The church can provide communities of love for both care givers and those in need of care. The Chicago Metro Synod of the Evangelical Lutheran Church of America has adopted for its parishes the model of "the congregation as healing place."

The foundation of all healing is the grace of the gospel. We are called to heal others out of the resources of grace that God has given. God's mercy-filled reality is bent to the relief of suffering. Jesus' ministry was empowered and sustained by the Spirit. Paul knew that apart from root-edness in God's love our greatest acts of sacrifice can be futile. We are free to minister healing to others when we have known the healing touch of God in our own lives. That healing in turn enables us to stand in solidarity with others who are suffering, to offer them a ministry of healing, and to grow in grace from the very people we seek to serve.

Sixth Sunday after the Epiphany

Lutheran	Roman Catholic	Episcopal	Common Lectionary
2 Kings 5:1-14	Lev. 13:1-2, 44-46	2 Kings 5:1-15b	2 Kings 5:1-14
1 Cor. 9:24-27	1 Cor. 10:31—11:1	1 Cor. 9:24-27	1 Cor. 9:24-27
Mark 1:40-45	Mark 1:40-45	Mark 1:40-45	Mark 1:40-45

FIRST LESSON: 2 KINGS 5:1-15

This passage features a miraculous deed of the prophet Elisha. Naaman was commander of the Syrian army. He had leprosy. Although it was apparently not severe enough to force him into isolation, he was shamed by it and concerned. On hearing about the prophet Elisha of Israel, Naaman decided to request a healing. He sent the request through the king of Syria to the king of Israel (a common procedure), without mentioning Elisha. He made the request despite the tense relations between Syria and Israel. The Israelite king balked, assuming that the Syrian king was simply seeking an excuse for war. Instead of calling for the miracle-working Elisha, the king responded that a king was no god to grant life and death.

Elisha, hearing of the request, took the initiative to offer healing, perhaps in order to get recognition for Yahweh from the Syrians. Naaman came with gifts, expecting Elisha to show him great deference and offer a dramatic display of healing. Instead Elisha, without leaving his house, simply directed Naaman to wash seven times in the river, the number seven symbolizing a complete healing. Naaman was offended and became irate, but his underlings, appealing to him as "father," convinced Naaman to follow the instructions. When he did, he was healed. Naaman returned to Elisha with his gifts (which Elisha refused) and declared, " 'Now I know that there is no God in all the earth except in Israel.' " (v. 15).

SECOND LESSON: 1 CORINTHIANS 9:24-27

First Corinthians deals with the relinquishment necessary to prevent division. This passage is the conclusion to chapter 9, which deals with Paul's relinquishment of his apostolic rights on behalf of those to whom he preaches the gospel (see previous lesson). Paul has been addressing people who do not want to give up their rights and freedoms as Christians. Paul must convince them to understand the importance of self-renunciation in order to serve others. To do so Paul draws on familar images from the ancient Isthmian games held annually near Corinth. He makes three key points.

First, the Corinthian Christians need to learn to sacrifice now for the sake of the future eschatological glory, which Paul believes will come soon. Paul has just indicated that he himself does everything for the sake of the gospel, so that "I may share in its blessings." To emulate Paul, the Corinthians should sacrifice for the future like athletes do. Athletes work out, discipline themselves, and pommel their bodies to put themselves in the best possible condition for the competitions. They do this in order to win the crown. Athletes also maintain a strict diet and refrain from sexual relations—sacrifices that were especially relevant to the issues in Corinth. The Corinthians should think of life as preparation for a contest and as the contest itself. They will need self-discipline and self-sacrifice in order to win a prize.

Second, the Corinthian Christians will not win merely by competing (v. 24). That only one person wins the crown is beside Paul's point. One will not win, Paul insists, simply because one has entered the race. One will have to sacrifice and exercise discipline to win. Therefore run in such a way that you might win, and not for a perishable crown at the games (made of celery stalks or date fronds) but for an imperishable crown of glory. Paul may also be encouraging self-renunciation for a group effort, such as relay races and team games. Thus each person will sacrifice for the benefit of the common good now, in order to participate in the common victory or salvation later.

Third, self-discipline maximizes one's effectiveness in the task at hand. The disciplined runner does not end up flailing the legs fruitlessly and the boxer does not box the air. When Paul preaches, he does not do so ineffectively. He gives the gospel free of charge, he relinquishes his apostolic rights to increase the credibility of the gospel, and he places himself in solidarity with those to whom he preaches. Without such "athletic" discipline, Paul might preach ineffectively or save others and then lose out himself.

All is rooted in the theology of the cross. Because the Lord gave his life for others, Paul gives himself, and thus should the Corinthians give themselves for one another.

GOSPEL: MARK 1:40-45

The cleansing of the leper displays God's rule over the arena of the unclean. Uncleanness is an important but neglected dimension of Mark's story. In order to grasp it we need to understand purity and pollution in Israel.

41

Israel's society was organized to preserve what was holy and to avoid what was unclean. This was in accordance with the command in the Torah: "Be holy for I am holy." Virtually every facet of life in Israel was labeled clean or unclean, pure or polluted, holy or defiled. For example, space was understood in terms of degrees of holiness, from the Holy of Holies in the temple to the court of the priests, the court of Israelites, the court of women, the court of the Gentiles, the city of Jerusalem, and the land of Israel, with gentile territory labeled unclean. People were also categorized according to degrees of holiness, from the high priest to the chief priests, the Levites, the Israelites, down to converts, slaves, and people with "deformities." Even time was arranged according to holiness, as with the Sabbath, the Passover, the Feast of Booths, the Day of Atonement, and so on.

The whole system was based on the notion that one achieved holiness by separation from what was unclean. God was separated within the temple, away from what defiled, and God might withdraw from the temple if unclean people entered it. Jews separated themselves from people and things that would defile them so as to keep their lives holy for the Lord. The chief priests and other Sadducees applied the purity rules to people only when they came to the temple. The Pharisees, by contrast, applied the purity rules to all Jews in the conviction that all Israel was a nation of priests. Thus, the Pharisees purified their hands and food before eating, and they avoided eating with unclean tax collectors and sinners, thereby indirectly avoiding contact with unclean Gentiles. In Mark we see the Pharisees protecting against defilement: condemning Jesus for eating with sinners, seeking to charge him for defiling the Sabbath, and attacking the disciples for eating with unclean hands.

Yet the Gospel of Mark sets the whole system in reverse. Instead of withdrawing to avoid uncleanness, Jesus and the disciples spread purity through the Holy Spirit. Instead of God withdrawing from the risk of defilement, God crosses the boundary from heaven and sends the Holy Spirit on Jesus. Instead of remaining isolated within the Holy of Holies, God splits the curtain of the sanctuary and leaves the temple in order to be available to people everywhere who pray the prayer of faith. Jesus does not separate from unclean people or things. On the contrary, he makes an onslaught on the arena of uncleanness. He touches a leper, drives out "unclean spirits," eats with tax collectors and sinners, heals on the Sabbath, touches a woman with a flow of blood, touches a corpse, drives out a legion of demons from a graveyard into a herd of pigs(!), and declares all foods clean.

Instead of becoming defiled by this contact, Jesus spreads purity and wholeness. Instead of becoming defiled by the woman with the flow of blood, Jesus heals her. Instead of being defiled by the corpse of the girl, Jesus raises her. Here is the spread of holiness rather than separation from impurity. The announcement that God's rule has arrived means that holiness is the active and powerful force and that uncleanness will be removed in its wake.

The story of the leper is paradigmatic. Lepers (people with ruptured skin, not the modern leprosy) were isolated from others. They were to stand so many paces away and warn people by calling out, "Unclean! Unclean!" The bold leper in this passage comes to Jesus, however, kneels before him, and pleads, " 'If you choose, you can make me clean.' " The leper does not want simply to be cured. He wants to be cleansed, so that he can be restored to his relationships in society. In response Jesus touches him and says, " 'I do choose. Be made cleansed!' " He was cleansed immediately. Instead of being defiled by contact with the leper, Jesus spreads holiness/wholeness. Then Jesus orders him to offer the sacrifice required of him and to get the priest to declare him officially clean so that he can return to a normal place in society. Jesus is concerned not only with a cure, but with the restoration of people to society.

At the end of the story the man spreads the word so broadly that Jesus is no longer able to enter a city openly but has to remain outside in deserted places.

HOMILETICAL REFLECTIONS

Two of the lessons are about crossing boundaries. Naaman crosses national and ethnic boundaries to reach Elisha. Jesus crosses a societal boundary to touch and heal the unclean leper. As we have seen, epiphanies reveal the nature of God. Here God is manifest as one who has compassion on all who are on the outside, one who crosses boundaries to reach the excluded, and one who seeks to include all.

There are basically two approaches to boundaries. We either set boundaries and guard them to protect ourselves or cross boundaries because they are too confining. In Mark the authorities raise boundary lines and guard them. They seek to keep some people out and protect those who are in. Mark, by contrast, is concerned with crossing boundaries. Jesus is a boundary-crossing figure. He crosses the line that separates clean from unclean. He crosses the line that isolates the lepers. He crosses the line that keeps out tax collectors and sinners. He crosses the line that keeps out Gentiles. Whereas society has erected boundaries to protect itself, Jesus crosses boundaries in order to reach people precisely because they are outside the boundaries.

Society's reaction to AIDS is a contemporary parallel. A prominent physician recently tried to establish a hospice for AIDS patients in a town in the East but was prohibited by the people of the town. We have seen many instances of such ill treatment. Instead of seeking safe contact with persons with AIDS, we prefer to avoid them altogether. Society needs to find ways to reach across lines to those in need. A church organization in New York City gives dietary advice and delivers three meals a day to homebound persons with AIDS. This organization serves thousands in the New York–New Jersey area. They call their group God Loves—We Deliver.

But our society shuns not only people with AIDS. Many different groups suffer open discrimination. People often have difficulty relating to those with disabilities of various kinds and so avoid them. Others avoid gays and lesbians because of their own feelings of discomfort. The list could go on. We justify ourselves with what we think are the best of reasons. In so doing, however, we help build society's boundaries, often without realizing it. We thereby cut off and isolate people. People with disabilities illustrate this tendency in society. They often literally do not have access.

People also set up boundaries between themselves and other races, ethnic groups, and social classes. We all have a tendency to surround ourselves with people like us. An honest look at ourselves may reveal how rarely we have meaningful contact with other people of a different social class or race. When the dominant culture avoids particular groups, these groups become isolated, limited to certain jobs, certain neighborhoods, certain social classes. The result is a permanent underclass that is unable to determine its own destiny (see John Kenneth Galbraith, *The Culture of Contentment* [Boston: Houghton Mifflin, 1992]). Society's tendency to ignore those who are on the outside further marginalizes them.

God is not a defensive being who withdraws from impurity, hardship, heartache, sin, or differentness. Jesus was not a figure who drew likeminded people into a safe haven to shut out the frightening things of life. Nor did the disciples establish a safe center and then invite people to come for renewal. On the contrary, the Gospels see God as an active force relating the Spirit directly to unclean spirits, lepers, women, the ill, prostitutes, tax collectors, and Gentiles—people on the margins or outside the boundaries of society. Jesus clearly identified all the people on the fringes of society and sought to place them at the center. At the same time these same marginalized Jews of Galilee courageously crossed boundaries to take the kingdom to the dominant Hellenized culture of the Roman Empire.

Surely we can foster enriching relationships with people who are different from us. Naaman, a Syrian officer, almost missed his healing because he did not think Elisha showed the proper deference or made a proper display for him. We should let neither arrogance nor fear keep us from crossing boundaries. The king of Israel, because of his fear, almost lost the opportunity to help an enemy and reconcile two nations. We need to quell the fear that prevents us from reaching out to those who are different from us. We must establish trust, however tenuous, and rekindle our belief, amid so much that divides us, in miracles of reconciliation.

The church has, unfortunately, been one of the last organizations in American society to bring together people of different cultures or social classes. Without any deliberate design, our church walls have become boundaries that attract for certain people inside and keep others outside. We need ways to cross the boundaries to reach others and at the same time to make our boundaries easy for others to cross. After all, our commitment to spread life rather than to cling to it is rooted in the epiphany of a God who has crossed the boundaries of heaven and earth to reach and befriend us.

Seventh Sunday after the Epiphany

Lutheran	Roman Catholic	Episcopal	Common Lectionary
Isa. 43:18-25	Isa. 43:18-19, 21-22, 24b-25	Isa. 43:18-25	Isa. 43:18-25
2 Cor. 1:18-22	2 Cor. 1:18-22	2 Cor. 1:18-22	2 Cor. 1:18-22
Mark 2:1-12	Mark 2:1-12	Mark 2:1-12	Mark 2:1-12

FIRST LESSON: ISAIAH 43:18-25

Israel is in exile in Babylon, away from the homeland, separated from the places and customs that gave them identity, certain that God has abandoned them. They are lost in captivity, banished to a strange place because they had broken the covenant. In these circumstances, they have forgotten God, abandoned God. But now Isaiah enters with a word of great promise from the Lord. Although the people broke the covenant, God did not. Although they have abandoned God, God has not abandoned them. Although they have forgotten God, God has not forgotten them.

Here God declares an incredible deliverance, so great that the Israelites will forget even the glorious exodus of the past and remember only this act of God. God may have made a way across the Red Sea, but now God will make a way across the vast, barren desert that separates the Israelites from their homeland. God will not merely provide occasional manna from heaven and water from rocks as in the desert with Moses. God will provide a road through this desert and create rivers to sustain the people. God will eliminate the threat from any wild animals. This is a new exodus with no hardships across the great desert toward a restored life in Palestine. This deliverance of Israel is promised in such a way as to imply that, for all intents and purposes, it is already accomplished.

Then the prophet recounts Israel's failings, charges laid out as by a prosecutor. The Israelites did not call on God, did not offer sacrifices, did not bring offerings, did not burn incense. They had given up on their relationship with God. Ironically the Lord says that he did not burden Israel with demands of sacrifices in exile—after all, God had destroyed the temple. Besides, what God really wanted was justice and mercy rather than sacrifice. In exile they might at least have honored God with justice. Instead they have burdened God with their sins, wearied God with their iniquities. What a reversal! God is no longer the master and the Israelites the slaves who carry the master's burdens. God has become the servant who carries the burdens of Israel.

Suddenly the charges are interrupted by the announcement of an executive pardon. Just because they have abandoned God does not mean God will do likewise. On the contrary, God is God. God forgives transgressions, blots out sins, forgets their offenses. God will do this not because Israel deserves it, for they deserve judgment. God will do it for God's own sake, because it is in God's character to be loyal, to forgive, to restore. Yet, in a sense, God really does do it for their sake, because God is being faithful to the divine tendency to express unmerited self-giving to those with whom God is in covenant.

SECOND LESSON: 2 CORINTHIANS 1:18-22

Paul is reestablishing his credibility after reneging on a promise to visit Corinth on his way from Macedonia to Jerusalem. He roots his trustworthiness in the faithfulness of God.

Paul had said he would visit Corinth on his way from Macedonia to Jerusalem with the offering for the church in Jerusalem. While in Ephesus of Asia Minor, however, he had to make an unexpected visit to Corinth to deal with a problem there, and he ran into trouble. The situation in Corinth was so bad that Paul withdrew rather than risk confrontation. As a result, he wrote a scathing letter to them. It was actually a "tearful letter" that indicated his grief and urged them to act against the offending party. Paul went on to Macedonia, but in light of the problems he had encountered in Corinth, he decided not to return to Corinth on his way from Macedonia to Jerusalem, as he had said he would. While still in Macedonia, however, Paul could hardly carry on his work because of his anxiety about the situation in Corinth, and so he sent Timothy to find out what was happening.

Meanwhile the Corinthians acted in Paul's favor to discipline the offending party. Yet some were now offended by Paul's letter and his decision not to return to Corinth. When Timothy returned with this news, Paul wrote another letter to explain his change of mind and to convince them of his concern for them. He reestablishes his credibility as a basis for his request that they participate in the collection for Jerusalem.

Paul reminds the Corinthians that he has dealt with them in sincerity and frankness and that they will be the source of glory for one another on the day of the Lord. Then Paul defends his integrity. Although he had appeared to say yes (he would visit Corinth) and then to say no (he would not), he can be counted on for his word because it is rooted in the gospel. Paul invites them to look at the faithfulness of God, whom Paul represents. In Jesus, God said nothing but yes to all God's promises. Paul had proclaimed the word of God to the Corinthians, and God had given the Spirit as a seal of the truth of that proclamation. The Spirit was also the down payment that guaranteed the complete fulfillment of God's promises in the future. The Corinthians themselves had affirmed all this with an *amen*. Thus the integrity of Paul's word about visits to Corinth is assured by God's faithfulness and God's confirmation of Paul's proclamation as an apostle.

Then Paul explains why he decided not to return. Paul was not insincere. He had simply changed his mind. Paul intended to visit when he first promised to. But after the urgent visit and the tearful letter, he wanted to spare the Corinthians further pain. Out of concern for them, he had withdrawn, because he did not want to force his will on them and perhaps split the community. Out of concern he had decided to spare them the pain his presence would cause them. He preferred not to relate to them as an authority figure but as a partner in joy. He could not stand to cause them sadness. Thus, even Paul's no was an affirmation—a yes of his love for them.

Paul assumes this letter will resolve the matter, for later in the letter he writes that he will visit them on the way to Jerusalem in the expectation that now they will contribute to the collection.

GOSPEL: MARK 2:1-12

The Gospel of Mark continues its display of the kingdom, showing Jesus' authority over sin. This healing story is interrupted by a conflict between Jesus and the scribes.

Jesus has returned home to his headquarters in Capernaum. On seeing the faith of the suppliants, Jesus says to the paralytic, " 'Son, your sins are forgiven.' " This is shocking. The temple system alone deals with the nation's sins when the high priest enters the Holy of Holies in the temple on the Day of Atonement to ask pardon for the sins of the people. Yet here is a Galilean teacher pardoning sins. The passive voice of the verb ("are forgiven") shows that God is the source of the pardon while Jesus is the one who declares it.

The scribes think this is blasphemy, a violation of God's sole right to forgive sins. By confining God to the ways God had acted in the past or to the established channels, they are mistaking the work of God in Jesus for blasphemy. This is dangerous for Jesus as well as for them. Blasphemy is punishable by death. In Mark blasphemy is the charge on which the Jewish authorities condemned Jesus to death. Throughout the story Jesus avoids indictment until the authorities pose the key question at his trial. Meanwhile their efforts to trap him escalate through a series of conflict stories until they go off to plot his destruction with the Herodians. When one puts new wine in old wineskins, one destroys the wine and the wineskins (see especially the Gospel lesson for the next week).

Jesus discerns in his spirit their internal accusations, and he asks them whether it it is easier to forgive or to heal. His question assumes the following: If sin is the cause of the illness and I remove the illness, then I have also forgiven the sin. Therefore forgiveness and healing are the same. Jesus is going to heal the man, but he wants the scribes to know that God has given to the Son of Humanity (Jesus) the authority to pardon sins. Actually God is still the one who pardons sins, but God has delegated this task to Jesus. Jesus then proceeds to heal the paralytic. Jesus has cleverly evaded indictment, for they can indict him for forgiving but they cannot indict him for healing.

The story again shows us that Jesus has authority and the scribes do not. Their lack of authority is evident in their failure to voice their objection openly, in their failure to see the new thing God is doing in Jesus, and the lack of power in their words in contrast to Jesus' declaration of pardon and of healing. Finally, their lack of authority is evident in their unwillingness to cheer the incredible healing that has taken place. A paralytic got up and walked! Because they are more concerned to guard God and God's laws, the authorities never celebrate the astounding wonders that the kingdom brings—demons defeated, illness eradicated, limbs restored, the unclean cleansed, and society healed. But the crowds respond appropriately. "We never saw anything like this." They are ready to follow Jesus to the sea and the desert in order to experience more of the reign of God.

HOMILETICAL REFLECTIONS

The lessons go to the heart of all epiphanies, for they attest to the unfailing goodness of God. In the Old Testament passage God is shown to be infinitely resourceful when it comes to faithfulness and goodness. When God has every reason to abandon the Israelites, God presents the most astounding offer of pardon and restoration. Time and again this happened for Israel. Despite the idolatry and apostasy of many Israelites, some Jews understood. And they could only sing the Lord's praises, that God's mercies were new every morning, that God's mercy endures forever.

The whole thrust of the good news is that God brings us to repentance by acts of goodness. This is what Paul knows so well. He declares in a kind of doxology that all the promises of God have their affirmation in Jesus. Jesus is God's *Yes!* to humanity. God is reliable. God can be counted on. God has justified people in Jesus, proclaimed salvation through the apostles, and given the Holy Spirit as assurance of more to come. Paul, caught by this goodness, saw his zeal to persecute Christians melt away. He had been transformed by "love poured out on his heart." All he cares about is to know Christ, the power of his resurrection, and the fellowship of his sufferings (Phil. 3:10).

The same good news pervades the Gospel story. The arrival of the kingdom is an explosion of divine self-giving, which generates human wholeness: forgiveness, blessing, healing, exorcism, cleansing, reconciliation, freedom, acceptance, hospitality. God pours God's being out on behalf of humanity. Notice that Jesus offers healing out of compassion, not as a display to gain followers. He heals with no strings attached. He does not ask the suppliant to believe something or to do something or even to follow him in exchange for the healing. In fact nowhere in Mark does Jesus ask anyone he heals to follow him. Healing is never done as a thinly disguised pretext for evangelism but because it is the right thing to do. So that they do not broadcast his healings as displays of power, Jesus tells people to be quiet or to go home—without control, without manipulation, out of the free self-giving of God.

In the Markan passage, Jesus addresses not only the illness but also the sinful root of the illness. The ancients believed that illness was a punishment for sin. We no longer take that position. Yet we could hardly deny that by our abuse of our bodies, our life-styles, and our disregard for the environment we have contributed to our current ill health. It is an expression of the goodness of God that Jesus addresses not just the results but also the root cause of illness, not just the paralysis but the sin, not just the leprosy but the uncleanness, not just the possession but the separation from family, and not just the blindness but the purpose in life. Ministering to the causes that lie behind an illness can be crucial to recovery and can bring renewal even when a cure does not take place.

In this way God's goodness enables our goodness. God loves us into loving. A teenage girl in Florida told her pastor that she could not forgive her parents. The pastor might have berated her for that. Instead he said, "Of course you cannot forgive until you have been healed of the hurt." As he subsequently ministered to her hurt, the girl came to forgive her parents. God is all yes. God forgives so we can forgive, heals so we can heal, shows mercy so we can show mercy, blesses so we can bless. Even the threats of the prophets and divine punishments are God's last-ditch efforts to bring people to their senses, to shake the foundations, to initiate a new beginning, to assure an ongoing covenant that is meaningful.

These lessons provide an opportunity to relish the goodness of God, which is shown in spontaneous acts of love for humanity. In turn, we are called to manifest God's yes to others. In *The John Wesley: Great Experiment* (Nashville: Discipleship Resources, 1965), Sam Teague offers a set of daily spiritual exercises that includes this one: Each day do "a totally *unselfish* and *unexpected* act of kindness or generosity." With this discipline, one experiences day after day the joy of participating in the spontaneous goodness of God. It is, indeed, "more blessed to give than to receive." What a blessing for everyone. As Shakespeare wrote, mercy is "twice bless'd: It blesseth him that gives and him that takes."

Such grace can undergird all of our actions. In whatever work we do or vocation we have, we can do more than is required or we can do it with special care and excellence, so that all is done not out of obligation but out of grace—even though one gets paid for it as a job! We can affirm even when we deny, as Paul did when he decided not to go to Corinth. We have a hard time saying yes to people at the same time we are constrained to say no to them. A teaching colleague of mine had to cast a difficult vote to expel a student, but then she sought him out to help him deal with the decision. She measured her relationships with her students by the respect and concern she offered those who did not pass her classes. She did not let her no to the behavior keep her from saying yes to the person. Likewise, God is for us even when against us. All is grace!

The biblical writers attest that grace and mercy are the deepest heart of God. The season of Epiphany celebrates the manifestation of God as mercy to human beings. It is a celebration that can overwhelm and transform.

Eighth Sunday after the Epiphany

Lutheran	Roman Catholic	Episcopal	Common Lectionary
Hos. 2:14-16, 19-20	Hos. 2:16b, 17b, 21-22	Hos. 2:14-23	Hos. 2:14-20
2 Cor. 3:1b-6	2 Cor. 3:1b-6	2 Cor. 3:17—4:2	2 Cor. 3:1-6
Mark 2:18-22	Mark 2:18-22	Mark 2:18-22	Mark 2:18-22

FIRST LESSON: HOSEA 2:14-23

God pointed out to Hosea (one of the eighth-century prophets) the similarity between the adultery of Hosea's wife and the apostasy of Israel in relation to God. God had commanded Hosea to take a woman of whoredom as his wife and to name his children No mercy and Not my people. His wife, Gomer, left him and went after other men. Despite this unfaithfulness, Hosea made the decision to bring her back and begin the marriage again. In marriages of the time, a husband had both authority over and love for the wife. As such, Hosea relates both the authority (justice) and the love of God (covenant loyalty) to the analogy: Yahweh will bring Israel back from apostasy to other gods and will renew the covenant relationship. Hosea gives the prophecy in such a way as to weave his personal story together with the God and Israel story.

Hosea expresses ambivalent feelings toward Gomer. He details her sins and threatens her with destruction, because she has forgotten her Lord. Yet in the next breath, he loves her and wants to woo her back to him. In fact it is because Israel has forgotten God that he will court her again. Precisely because Israel has failed in the covenant, God refuses to be like that and will not let her go. Thus, on the one hand, God threatens to destroy Israel if she will not stop her apostasy. On the other hand, God promises to renew the relationship without conditions or punishment.

A series of scenes outlines Hosea's plan to court Gomer again. God will court Israel (as in Egypt), bring her through the desert as in the days of old (the wandering), and speak to her heart. He will give her a betrothal gift of vineyards (the land), and he will make the valleys of Achor (an obstacle to the first conquest of the land) into a "door of hope." Then the exchange of covenant vows will take place, and Israel will address the Lord as her husband rather than as her master, and she will renounce all relationships with other gods (Baals). On behalf of Israel, God will cut a covenant with the wild animals in the land, abolish the threat of war, and enable Israel to live securely in the land. The Lord pledges to the marriage righteousness, justice, covenant loyalty, and mercy. In return Israel will no longer forget the Lord but will know God in faithfulness and trust. When this happens, the heavens will give rain, the earth its harvest, and the children will be renamed Mercy and My people.

SECOND LESSON: 2 CORINTHIANS 3:1-6

(For 2 Cor. 3:17—4:2, see Last Sunday after the Epiphany.)

Paul reasserts his authority as a basis for asking the Corinthians to participate in the collection for Jerusalem (chapters 8 and 9). He has reassured them that he cares about them despite his canceled visit. In a dialogical style of question and answer, he now defends his apostleship.

Other Christian missionaries, perhaps apostles, have come to Corinth and functioned differently from Paul. They accepted the hospitality of the Corinthians and perhaps received financial support from them. They came bearing letters of recommendation and planned to request letters from the Corinthians to introduce themselves to other communities. As a result, the Corinthians doubted Paul, because Paul had refused hospitality and support from the Corinthians: Was he acting like a real apostle? Neither had Paul offered or asked for letters of recommendation: Was he recommending himself? Does this reflect true apostleship?

Paul begins the defense of his apostleship with an image of the role of an apostle: a triumphal procession led by God with the apostles spreading the fragrance that comes of knowing God. This knowledge of God proffered by the apostles brings life to those who receive it and death to those who do not. Then Paul asks: Who is sufficient to such a task? Certainly not those who peddle the gospel out of greed. By contrast, says Paul, we are sincere, sent by God, living in Christ, and standing in the presence of God.

Then, in this pericope, Paul shows his awareness that people will misinterpret what he is saying as self-commendation. With a measure of sarcasm, he says: Surely we do not need letters of recommendation from you or to you, do we? From Paul's point of view, he hardly needs to commend himself. He founded the Christian community in Corinth. When he arrived, there was no Christian community to receive a letter of recommendation. And it would be strange now for Paul to get a letter from a church he had founded. Everyone knows that Paul was responsible for the founding of the community at Corinth. This fact is public. It can be known and "read" by all. Is that not recommendation enough? The Corinthians are his letter of recommendation, authored by Christ, penned by Paul, with the ink of the Spirit, and written on their hearts. Paul does not visit churches; he founds them. He is an apostle, and the existence of the Corinthian community proves it.

Paul then emphasizes that the competence and sufficiency of an apostle comes from Christ, not from credentials or from letters of recommendation. God is the source; Christ and the Spirit are the means. Paul's success is possible because he is minister of a new covenant written with the Spirit, which brings life, and not on stone tablets, which bring death. God has written his letter of recommendation on the hearts of the Corinthian Christians. Cannot the Corinthians see that they themselves are Paul's recommendation and listen to him as an authentic apostle?

GOSPEL: MARK 2:18-22

This is the key episode at the center of a series of five conflict stories set in Galilee. The five stories form a concentric ring pattern (A B C B' A'). Many similarities exist between A (healing of a paralytic) and A' (healing of a withered hand) and between B (eating with tax collectors) and B' (eating on the Sabbath). The key to the series is our central episode, C (on fasting), for it explains all the conflict stories: The authorities are judging the new wine of Jesus with the old wineskins of the laws and traditions.

The episode itself has a two-part question and a two-part answer. Some people (unidentified) ask Jesus why the disciples of John and of the Pharisees fast but his disciples do not. The first part of Jesus' reply explains why his disciples do not fast in contrast to John's disciples, and the second part explains why Jesus' disciples do not fast in contrast with the disciples of the Pharisees.

In order to understand Jesus' reply, we need to understand his use of parables. Mark's parables are not simple stories meant to clarify what is obscure. Nor are they subversive stories with one point of impact. Rather they are riddlelike allegories that explain Jesus' actions in the larger story of the Gospel.

In the first part of his answer, Jesus shows why he does not fast in relation to John's disciples. This first allegory about the bridegroom shows that John's disciples fast now because John has been taken from them. Jesus' disciples, by contrast, do not fast because Jesus is still with them. Like the attendants of a bridegroom, they are not permitted to fast, for they are to celebrate. When Jesus is taken from them, then they will fast. At times we suspend traditional customs for more important tasks and opportunities.

In the second part of his answer, Jesus explains why he does not fast in contrast with the Pharisees. Here are the parallels:

Allegory	Applied to Jesus
New patch	Jesus, the kingdom
Old garment	Laws and customs
Pulls away	Do not mix
Rip gets worse	Situation gets worse

Jesus is saying: Do not try to fit this new reality of the kingdom into traditional laws and customs. Otherwise the situation that the kingdom came to correct will get worse.

Then Jesus repeats the same point in another allegory. Here are the parallels:

Allegory	Applied to Jesus
Do not put	Do not judge
New wine	Jesus, the kingdom
Into old wineskins	By laws and traditions
Wine bursts wineskins	Newness explodes laws and customs
Wine and wineskins are destroyed	Both Jesus and the traditions are destroyed

Here the point is that people are not to judge Jesus by the old traditions. Jesus acts outside the temple, outside the synagogue, outside the traditions, outside the traditional interpretations of the law, outside the urban elite, outside the holy city. Jesus and the kingdom are new and will not fit into the old standards. If people judge by those standards, they will destroy Jesus and the traditional institutions as well.

Now we can see how this point is the centerpiece of the five conflict stories and the key teaching that explains all these conflicts. A: It is inappropriate to judge Jesus' pardon of sins by traditional views of blasphemy. B: It is inappropriate to fit Jesus' eating with sinners into the custom of exclusive table fellowship. C: It is incorrect to judge Jesus' fasting practices by the practices of the Pharisees. B': It is wrong to judge the picking of grain on the Sabbath by the current interpretation of the Sabbath. A': It is hardness of heart to seek to indict Jesus for healing on the Sabbath.

Do not put new wine into old wineskins. Rather put new wine into new wineskins. Otherwise both wine and wineskins will be destroyed. Unfortunately Jesus' plea went unheeded. The Pharisees continued to put new wine into old wineskins in the very next two conflicts after this teaching (B' and A'). At the end of the series of five episodes, the Pharisees go off and plot with the Herodians to destroy Jesus (3:6). Later Jesus predicts that God will destroy the tenants of the vineyard for not bearing fruit and will destroy the temple for not being a house of prayer for Gentiles. In the end Jesus' prediction was correct: The wine (Jesus) was destroyed and so were the wineskins (institutions of Israel).

55

HOMILETICAL REFLECTIONS

The lessons show that God works in new ways and outside official channels. Epiphanies come from surprising sources. When traditional institutions failed, God worked outside them. When national institutions were not fruitful, God sent the prophets. When the temple system did not work, God anointed the Galilean Messiah. When the apostles had not yet left Jerusalem, God raised up Paul as apostle to the Gentiles. God has an infinite variety of ways to be manifest in the world and is not limited to working through Israel or the church. God's epiphanies come in new and often unexpected ways.

In each lesson the agent of God has difficulty establishing credibility. People do not readily accept prophets or apostles or messiahs, because these figures do not have the authority of custom and institution. In each lesson the one who speaks for God seeks to explain the message so it will be heard. Hosea acts out his prophecy. Paul defends his apostolic actions. Jesus clarifies his purposes. The problem is, How can people know God is at work when the agent does not bear official authorization? Will we be able to discern where God is at work when God is working in new ways and outside official channels? How do we distinguish between true and false epiphanies?

Hosea's prophecy is a wonderful story of God's love and fidelity. But it carries with it a raging condemnation of the nation as whores and adulterers. Hosea condemns those who have a vested interest in keeping the system going and who probably believe it is not all that bad. They were likely not pleased. Surely people should not take seriously anyone who talks like Hosea, especially someone whose own family life leaves much to be desired. Nearly three thousand years later we can readily see who was right and who was wrong. But would we have listened to Hosea as he called from outside the establishment? Do we now?

On what basis, then, would we determine whether Hosea's prophecy was a true manifestation of God? For Hosea the key seemed to be that he spoke of God's fidelity to Israel. God would love Israel despite all and would offer once more to restore Israel. Hosea did not relish destruction and condemnation. He would not let his desire for revenge prevail. Furthermore the integrity of his own fidelity to Gomer reinforced the authenticity of his message about God. What an experience of God's covenant loyalty this prophet must have had in order to bear such love for Israel/Gomer! This prophecy has its own intrinsic authority.

Paul functioned on the fringes of the official church in Jerusalem. He was unorthodox in his beliefs, methods, and practices. One often has the impression that Paul experienced Christ, received the Spirit, and then innovated in response to each new situation. Like the Corinthians, we might be suspicious of someone who does something for nothing. We might want credentials. Yet Paul's authority from God rested not in any title or degree but in the intrinsic worth of the work and word itself.

How do we know God was working through Paul? Paul announced a life of relinquishment for others. Christ had given his life for them. Therefore they were called to give their life for one another. The fragrance Paul preached brought life to those who breathed it in. Again, the integrity of Paul's own life bore the grace he preached. He did not exercise his full rights. He gave the gospel free of charge. He asked for money not for himself but for "the poor in Jerusalem." He did not relish domination but sought to create a serving community. What lengths he went to in order to lead people to hear the gospel! What lengths God has gone to in order to bring us salvation! Paul's authority rested on the intrinsic worth of his message in word and deed.

Jesus ministered outside the established institutions and customs. Surely someone who claimed to pardon sins, associated with tax collectors, disregarded the fasting customs, disobeyed the Sabbath, and reinterpreted the law could not be acting on God's behalf (let alone be a messiah). But this new reality required new ways of seeing. How did people recognize that Jesus was from God? As with Hosea and Paul, Jesus' authority was intrinsic. Jesus proclaimed good news of rescue for those in need. Jesus did not aggrandize himself. He healed without attaching obligations. He did acts of power and told people to be quiet about them. He preached service and he lived service. He proclaimed relinquishment and he gave up his life. His life was an extravagant expenditure of grace for those in need.

How do these lessons enable us to recognize authentic epiphanies of God today? God's work has its own intrinsic power to win our hearts. We either get it or we do not. In the movie *Oh God!*, no one would take Jerry (the character played by John Denver) seriously because surely God would not appear to a grocery clerk! Surely God would not become incarnate as a bellhop or a nursery attendant or a taxi driver (or a Galilean carpenter). Would we get it? Based on Hosea and Paul and the Son of God, we can be sure that God is seeking us out to deliver us from either our wayward ways or our deep needs. Are we open to see the ways God might reach us? If God sent the Messiah today, would we recognize her? Or would our prejudices, our loyalties, and our customs prevent us from seeing God at work where we did not expect it. God is manifest in the new, in the unexpected, in the challenges to tradition, and in the dislodging of our sin. We do well to pay attention.

The Transfiguration of Our Lord
Last Sunday after the Epiphany

Lutheran	Roman Catholic	Episcopal	Common Lectionary
2 Kings 2:1-12a	Dan. 7:9-10, 13-14	1 Kings 19:9-18	2 Kings 2:1-12a
2 Cor. 3:12—4:2	2 Pet. 1:16-19	2 Pet. 1:16-19	2 Cor. 4:3-6
Mark 9:2-9	Mark 9:2-10	Mark 9:2-9	Mark 9:2-9

FIRST LESSON: 2 KINGS 2:1-12a

This episode recounts the transfer of power from Elijah to Elisha, when Elijah is taken up into heaven and Elisha becomes his successor. Elisha is the leader of a group of prophets at Gilgal. As Elisha and Elijah are traveling down from Gilgal to Bethel, Elijah asks Elisha not to go with him any farther. Elisha knows that Elijah is about to die, and he takes an oath (repeatedly) that he will not leave Elijah. Elisha follows Elijah to Bethel then through Jericho on down to the Jordan River. Elijah miraculously parts the water with his mantle (a cape or loose-fitting cloak) and they both cross over. This threshold event is reminiscent of the Exodus crossing of the Red Sea and of the crossing of the Jordan in preparation to occupy the land.

Elisha asks Elijah for a double portion of the Spirit of God that had been on Elijah. Elisha asks this not in order to outdo Elijah but because this is the portion of inheritance an elder son would receive in contrast to the younger sons. In this way Elisha is asking to be the true successor of Elijah, to become the father of the sons of the prophets. Elijah promises that the request will be granted if Elisha sees him being taken up to God. (Elijah is the only figure in the Hebrew Bible to be taken up like this.) If Elisha sees this exit, he will have proven himself capable of discerning spiritual realities and will thus be worthy to receive Elijah's Spirit. Elisha does, indeed, see Elijah ascend. As Elijah goes, Elisha describes the theophany of chariots and horsemen that he sees and he addresses Elijah as father, signifying that the request will be granted. Elisha then picks up Elijah's mantle and uses it to recross the Jordan, just as Elijah had done.

SECOND LESSON: 2 CORINTHIANS 3:12—4:2

Paul has been explaining why he decided not to revisit Corinth on his return from Macedonia as he had promised to do. Here he argues that his boldness to make such decisions stems from the nature of the new covenant in Christ.

Paul depicts the nature of his bold ministry in the new covenant by contrasting it with the ministry of Moses in the old covenant. In the old covenant, God gave the law to Moses on Mount Sinai, and people were expected to obey it. In that covenant, God did not give people the resources to carry out their part of the covenant, to carry out the law. Because the covenant contained death penalties for noncompliance, people were liable for any penalties of law. Therefore Paul depicts the old covenant as a covenant of death. Clearly for Paul the old covenant was glorious, but its glory was one that fades, for God meant that covenant to be temporary until Christ and the Spirit came. As such, the old covenant of law was destined eventually to be invalidated and replaced.

As for the ministry of the old covenant, Paul says that Moses knew it was temporary. For this reason, in Paul's peculiar interpretation of this passage, Moses put a veil over his face when he turned to the Israelites in order to hide from them the fact that the glory of this covenant was fading. Moses did this as a minister of the old covenant, for otherwise the Israelites would have been disappointed and discouraged over the temporary nature of the covenant they were receiving. In Paul's view the result of this concealment by Moses was unfortunate: When the new covenant came, the hearts of many in Israel were hardened, because they mistakenly believed the old covenant was permanent and were unwilling to let go of it for the new covenant in Christ.

By contrast, Paul argues, the new covenant is vastly superior. In the new covenant God provides the resources for people to carry out God's will through the justification wrought in Christ. God gives empowerment through the Spirit and writes God's will on the heart. In contrast to the old covenant, the new covenant is permanent. Instead of a glory that fades, an even greater glory, toward a final consummation of glory, is guaranteed by the gift of the Spirit. In this covenant the ministers do not need to provide a veil, for they can lead people to look face-to-face at the Lord, the Spirit. When Moses had turned to the Lord, the veil was removed and his own face was transformed. Because the new covenant is permanent, everyone may see the Lord the Spirit in this way, face-to-face, and be transformed by the experience.

To behold God is to be transformed. To behold God is to see the splendor of God reflected in one's own self as in a mirror. Such a transformation from glory to glory restores human beings to their original creation in the image of God—the image of Christ. It remains then for people of the old covenant to "turn to the Lord," to repent and face the Lord, the Spirit. Then the veil is removed and they are converted (transformed) by the experience. Here there is freedom, for people are freed from outward regulations and they experience firsthand the empowering reality of God.

This nature of the new covenant has given Paul his boldness. Unlike Moses, who could not be bold because he had to hide the nature of the covenant in order to protect the Israelites, Paul has every reason to be bold and open. Paul proclaims a gospel in which the Spirit empowers and gives hope of greater, permanent glories. The Spirit empowers Paul's ministry and gives him confidence to do whatever he needs to do so that the people will not lose out on the glories of this covenant. That is why Paul could decide to visit Corinth and then change his mind when he thought a visit would be too painful for them. Paul was neither hypocritical nor negligent. Rather he was acting out of care and commitment to the Corinthians as a bold minister of a new covenant.

Paul is a fellow Jew of those in the old covenant. They worship the same God and share the same Scripture. Yet Paul believes that God has done a new thing in Christ. In light of this new thing Paul reconceives the Scripture in a distinctly Christian way. For Paul a veil has been removed in reading; he therefore sees in Scripture the temporary nature of the covenant of law under Moses. In light of his own experience of God and the Spirit, Paul sees himself and early Christians as encountering in some immediate way the reality of God, which frees from law and is a source of profound human transformation.

GOSPEL: MARK 9:2-9

The transfiguration story marks a transition from a Galilean ministry of miracles to a journey toward death in Jerusalem, a transition from Epiphany to Lent. As such, it manifests the relation between glory and suffering.

The transfiguration can be understood only in light of what precedes it. The transfiguration takes place just after Jesus' first teaching about suffering and death. Jesus told his disciples that he would "suffer greatly, be rejected by the elders, the high priests and the scribes, be put to death, and after three days rise." Peter's response was to rebuke Jesus. In turn, Jesus rebuked Peter: " 'You are setting your mind not on divine things but on human things.' "

He then told the disciples and the crowd, " 'If any want to become my followers, let them deny themselves and take up their cross and follow me.' " Then he gives the reason: " 'For those who want to save their life will lose it, and those who lose their life for my sake, and for the sake of the gospel, will save it.' " If people want to save their lives, they will lose them when the Son of Humanity shuns them when he comes in the glory of his Father. Conversely, if they lose their lives for Jesus and the good news, they will save them. The author of Mark believed that this event of the kingdom coming in power would take place before the generation was over (9:1).

Then Jesus takes along his inner circle of three disciples to a high mountain. It is six days later, the number six perhaps symbolizing a time just before the consummation (symbolized by the number seven, the number of completion). It is on a mountain, in the (lower) heavens near to God. It is an epiphany: The brightness, the cloud, and the voice are all manifestations of God's presence. It is also private; afterward Jesus tells his disciples not to recount what has happened until after the Son of Humanity has risen from the dead.

Jesus is transfigured before them. Although the word *glory* is not used, the description of the dazzling white clothes makes it clear that Jesus is being glorified. The point of Mark's story is not that a veil has been lifted to allow us to see the glory that has been there all the time. Rather the event foreshadows the glory that the Father will give to Jesus when Jesus "comes in the glory of his Father with the holy angels" (v. 38). The disciples are allowed to glimpse this glory ahead of time. Such a proleptic event of glory confirms for the disciples that they should believe Jesus' talk about death. For the very Jesus who will be rejected is the one who will also come as savior and judge at the end time.

The transfiguration experience clarifies to the disciples that Jesus is vastly superior to Moses and Elijah, who appear with Jesus and talk with him. The return of these two great figures of Jewish history was often associated with the end time. Peter and the other two disciples are terrified and want to make a booth to honor and protect them. The point of the episode is not so much that the disciples want to prolong some mountaintop experience but that they mistakenly treat all three as equals. Remember that the crowds thought Jesus was Elijah or a prophet (Moses) or John the Baptist (an Elijah type). The disciples had repeated these views just before Peter confessed Jesus as the Messiah. After Moses and Elijah appear with Jesus before the disciples, a cloud comes and a voice addresses the disciples: " 'This is my Son, the Beloved,' " that is, *"Only* this one is my beloved son." Then the voice (God) adds, "Listen to him." When the cloud goes away, they see only Jesus. To the disciples who had rebuked Jesus when he spoke of his death, God announces that Jesus is God's only son and that they should listen to him.

HOMILETICAL REFLECTIONS

The lessons depict epiphanies of glory. Elisha sees Elijah taken up to heaven. Paul experiences the Spirit as a foretaste of the final glorification of believers. The disciples witness a transfiguration foreshadowing Jesus' ultimate glorification. Jesus himself experiences transfiguration. Transfiguration is the ultimate epiphany, the manifestation of God in human beings. Such glorification of humans is not a matter of their trying to ascend to God in some spiritual quest. It is God manifesting glory to or in humans so that they become fully human, as they were meant to be.

In Mark glory from God confirms the Messiah who suffers and dies in the service of others. The glory of the transfiguration comes just after Jesus had prophesied his death. It confirms that the one who will be scorned is the one who speaks for God. Likewise the glory of the resurrection comes just after the crucifixion. It confirms that the one who lived and died this way is the one whom God honors. In the same way the return of Christ in glory comes after followers have given their lives for the good news. It confirms that all who follow Jesus in suffering service will prevail. Thus, the transfiguration of Jesus confirms for the disciples (and indirectly for the readers) that Jesus is the one who will judge humanity at the end time. Therefore heed him now.

The glory of the transfiguration, the resurrection, and the return in power confirm the life Jesus lived. In Jesus we see the definitive figure in history, the human being whom God created humanity to be. Like Elijah, Jesus was a wonder-worker. He healed leprosy, exorcised demons, and calmed the waters. Like Moses, he provided manna in the desert. But Jesus was more than Elijah. Jesus had full power from God, and he gave it all up for others. Jesus was more than the teacher and prophet Moses. Jesus had the authority of the Spirit to inaugurate God's kingdom, and he lived in service to others until death. Jesus is the full expression of humanity in God's image.

In turn, the Spirit of Jesus is given to believers so that they might reflect the same glory of Jesus in their lives. " 'If any want to become my followrs, let them deny themselves and take up their cross and follow me.' " In Mark to follow Jesus is to be like Jesus, to heal as he healed, to serve as he served, to give our lives as he gave his. The minor characters in Mark serve as examples: the suppliants who bring others for healing; the widow who gives out of her need; the Syrophoenician woman who humbles herself for her daughter; Simon, who takes up Jesus' cross; and Joseph of Arimathea, who risks arrest to bury Jesus. Today there are countless Markan Christians in the world who risk status, economic security, power, and life itself to care for and advocate for others. The glory of the transfiguration confirms that this is the life God wants us to live for others.

Mark's theology has been characterized as "glory through suffering." But this is misleading. Mark focuses less on suffering than on service: glory through service to the point of death. We are not to suffer for its own sake. Rather we lose our lives for Jesus and the good news. Nor are we to suffer in order to obtain glory. Followers are to serve others because it is the right thing to do, and they will be glorified.

Thus, the suffering that the transfiguration confirms is suffering that comes in the course of following Jesus. The transfiguration does not confirm suffering that results from illness. God wills to relieve this suffering, as the healings in Mark attest. Nor does the transfiguration confirm suffering that results from natural disaster. God wills to prevent these, as the rescues from storms and hunger in the desert attest. These sufferings are not our cross to bear. The suffering that the transfiguration confirms results from the choice to follow Jesus—to risk a reputation to advocate for someone, to give up our power so others can have power, to give to the poor out of our financial need, or to lose our dreams to care for another. These are the crosses that the transfiguration confirms.

To seek glory and honor from people is to seek greatness, power, acquisition, security for ourselves. To seek glory and honor from God is to give up the quest for human glory and to risk life, reputation, loss of power, and economic insecurity in service to others for Jesus and the good news. In God's eyes this is true human greatness. This is the glory of living. This is the living that glorifies God. This is the living that God glorifies. This glory from God is the ultimate epiphany—not just the glory of God revealed to people but the glory of God revealed in people.

To lose our lives for Jesus and the good news runs contrary to our natural instincts and our deepest desires for ourselves. The aim of the gospel is to liberate our self-centeredness and to enable us to serve others for God. Our capacity to do this is a response to glory given as a gift, a gift that enables us to reflect glory. Elisha's vision of Elijah gave him the power to become the father of the sons of the prophets. Paul knew that Christians give themselves as a response to the liberation of justification and the power of the Spirit. So too the disciples of Mark would eventually embrace the cost of Christ's passion because they had beheld the glories of Christ's Epiphany.

For Further Reading

THE GOSPEL OF MARK

Achtemeier, Paul. *Invitation to Mark*. Garden City, N.Y.: Doubleday, 1978.

Best, Ernest. *Mark: The Gospel as Story*. Edinburgh: T. & T. Clark, 1983.

Juel, Donald. *Mark*. Augsburg Commentary on the New Testament. Minneapolis: Augsburg, 1990.

Kelber, Werner. *Mark's Story of Jesus*. Philadelphia: Fortress Press, 1979.

Kingsbury, Jack. *Conflict in Mark: Jesus, Authorities, Disciples*. Minneapolis: Fortress Press, 1989.

Pallares, José Cárdenas. *A Poor Man Called Jesus: Reflections on the Gospel of Mark*. Maryknoll, N.Y.: Orbis, 1990.

Rhoads, David and Donald Michie. *Mark as Gospel: An Introduction to the Narrative of a Gospel*. Philadelphia: Fortress Press, 1982.

Waetjan, Herman. *A Reordering of Power: A Socio-Political Reading of Mark's Gospel*. Minneapolis: Fortress Press, 1989.

THE CORINTHIAN CORRESPONDENCE

Conzelmann, Hans. *1 Corinthians*. Hermeneia. Philadelphia: Fortress Press, 1975.

Danker, Frederick. *2 Corinthians*. Augsburg Commentary on the New Testament. Minneapolis: Augsburg, 1989.

Furnish, Victor Paul. *The Moral Teaching of Paul: Selected Issues*. Second edition. Nashville: Abingdon Press, 1985.

Harrisville, Roy. *1 Corinthians*. Augsburg Commentary on the New Testament. Minneapolis: Augsburg, 1987.

Roetzel, Calvin. *The Letters of Paul: Conversations in Context*. Third edition. Louisville: Westminster/John Knox, 1991.

Talbert, Charles. *Reading Corinthians: A Literary and Theological Commentary on 1 and 2 Corinthians*. New York: Crossroad, 1989.

Theissen, Gerd. *The Social Setting of Pauline Christianity: Essays on Corinth*. Philadelphia: Fortress Press, 1982.